Praise for
Does Your Broker Owe You Money?

"A candid look at the business of buying investment advice. Believe me, it isn't pretty." **—Jonathan Clements, *The Wall Street Journal***

"Solin's writing is clear. . . . His legal background offers a perspective rarely found in investment books." **—*BetterInvesting Magazine***

"[A] bold new book." **—*The San Diego Union-Tribune***

"Enable[s] the average investor to avoid being victimized. . . . This book is required reading for all brokerage house clients."

—William J. Bernstein, author of
The Intelligent Asset Allocator
and *The Four Pillars of Investing*

THE
SMARTEST
INVESTMENT BOOK
YOU'LL EVER READ

THE SIMPLE, STRESS-FREE WAY TO
REACH YOUR INVESTMENT GOALS

Daniel R. Solin

A PERIGEE BOOK

A PERIGEE BOOK
Published by the Penguin Group
Penguin Group (USA) Inc.
375 Hudson Street, New York, New York 10014, USA
Penguin Group (Canada), 90 Eglinton Avenue East, Suite 700, Toronto, Ontario M4P 2Y3, Canada
(a division of Pearson Penguin Canada Inc.)
Penguin Books Ltd., 80 Strand, London WC2R 0RL, England
Penguin Group Ireland, 25 St. Stephen's Green, Dublin 2, Ireland (a division of Penguin Books Ltd.)
Penguin Group (Australia), 250 Camberwell Road, Camberwell, Victoria 3124, Australia
(a division of Pearson Australia Group Pty. Ltd.)
Penguin Books India Pvt. Ltd., 11 Community Centre, Panchsheel Park, New Delhi—110 017, India
Penguin Group (NZ), Cnr. Airborne and Rosedale Roads, Albany, Auckland 1310, New Zealand
(a division of Pearson New Zealand Ltd.)
Penguin Books (South Africa) (Pty.) Ltd., 24 Sturdee Avenue, Rosebank, Johannesburg 2196,
South Africa

Penguin Books Ltd., Registered Offices: 80 Strand, London WC2R 0RL, England

While the author has made every effort to provide accurate telephone numbers and Internet addresses at the time of publication, neither the publisher nor the author assumes any responsibility for errors, or for changes that occur after publication. Further, the publisher does not have any control over and does not assume any responsibility for author or third-party websites or their content.

First edition: November 2006

Library of Congress Cataloging-in-Publication Data

Solin, Daniel R.
    The smartest investment book you'll ever read / Daniel R. Solin.
        p. cm.
    Includes index.
    ISBN 0-399-53283-8
    1. Investments. I. Title.
    HG4521.S71195 2006
    332.67'8—dc22

                                    2006043611

PRINTED IN THE UNITED STATES OF AMERICA

10 9 8 7 6 5 4 3 2 1

PUBLISHER'S NOTE: This publication is designed to provide accurate and authoritative information in regard to the subject matter covered. It is sold with the understanding that the publisher is not engaged in rendering legal, accounting, or other professional services. If you require legal advice or other expert assistance, you should seek the services of a competent professional. Continued on page 169.

Most Perigee Books are available at special quantity discounts for bulk purchases for sales promotions, premiums, fund-raising, or educational use. Special books, or book excerpts, can also be created to fit specific needs. For details, write: Special Markets, The Berkley Publishing Group, 375 Hudson Street, New York, New York 10014.

To hardworking investors. There is a better, easier, less stressful way to achieve your financial goals. I hope the time you spend reading this book will be the best investment you will ever make.

CONTENTS

PART THREE
SMART INVESTORS KNOW BETTER

PART FOUR
THE REAL WAY SMART INVESTORS BEAT 95 PERCENT OF THE "PROS"

THE
SMARTEST
INVESTMENT BOOK
YOU'LL EVER READ

PART ONE

BECOME A SMART INVESTOR: CHANGE YOUR INVESTMENT LIFE FOREVER

1

An Unbelievable Chimp Story

The investor's chief problem—and even his worst enemy—is likely to be himself.

—Benjamin Graham, author of *The Intelligent Investor*

There is a chimpanzee in a remote region of Sierra Leone that routinely performs open-heart surgery. His success rate is higher—and his mortality rate lower—than many of the finest heart surgeons in the world.

I made that up.

But if you read that report in the newspaper, you would think that either:

1. That chimp is really extraordinary; or
2. Those heart surgeons are not very good.

If the story were true, and you needed a heart operation, you might seek out the chimp and avoid the heart surgeons.

The *Financial Times* of London annually runs a contest, pitting a neophyte investor against market analysts. In 2002, a five-year-old London girl chose stocks randomly from one hundred pieces of paper listing companies on the *Financial Times* Stock Exchange. Her results were compared to those of a top financial analyst and those of a woman who used the "movement of the planets" to choose her portfolio.

Over a period of one year, the little girl won handily. Very handily, as a matter of fact. Her stocks gained 5.8 percent. In stark contrast, the portfolio of the professional analyst lost 46.2 percent. The analyst was also bested by the financial astrologer, whose stocks lost only 6.2 percent.

The little girl celebrated by going to McDonald's. I suspect the analyst continued to dine at more expensive establishments.

There are some excellent peer-reviewed studies that demonstrate that the stocks most highly rated by financial analysts consistently *underperform* the market.

Those reports are fact.

Either the little girl is very good, the analysts are very bad or the much-touted skill of stock picking is not something that any smart investor would want to bet the farm on.

And the chimp? Well, he still doesn't perform open-heart surgery.

2

An Unbelievable True Story

Most individual investors would be better off in an index mutual
fund.

—Peter Lynch, former manager of the Fidelity Magellan Fund,
Barron's, April 2, 1990

There are 100 million individual investors in the United States. They hold $8 trillion of stocks. More than $7.5 trillion of this money is invested the *wrong* way—by **money managers** who engage in what I call "hyperactive management": trying to "beat the market" by picking winners and timing the market. **This is dumb money**.

In sharp contrast, *trillions* of dollars of assets of pensions, foundations and university endowments are invested the *right* way—by money managers who seek market returns by investing in all of the stocks and bonds in broad market indexes. **This is smart money**.

Ironically, investing for market returns—being among the smart money—is much easier than investing hyperactively, because:

- You don't have to pay any attention to the financial media.
- You don't have to sift though mountains of often-conflicting and confusing information from self-styled experts.
- It is less expensive.

> **MONEY MANAGERS** are professionals who invest money on behalf of others. They take funds from individuals, pension funds, foundations and other endowments and invest it in markets according to particular criteria. Money managers are usually paid based on a percentage of the total money they invest. Therefore, if their investments make money and the pool of money they invest grows, so does their income.

- The results are demonstrably superior.
- The vast majority of investors do not need *any* advisor or broker. You can deal directly with brand-name mutual fund families or use Exchange Traded Funds (ETFs).
- It should take you only ninety minutes or so a year.

Why then does such a gap exist between the investing strategy of smart money and the way most individual investors invest? It is because most investors use financial consultants employed by the major brokerage firms or independent financial advisors who earn commissions or fees for selling financial products.

Virtually all of these brokerage-based financial consultants and most independent financial advisors manage money using dumb-money management techniques. They engage in **market timing** and **stock picking** because doing so makes them money.

THE TRUTH ABOUT DUMB MONEY INVESTING

Most financial advisors who work within this dumb-money system believe they have the ability to choose stocks and mutual funds that will outperform most other stocks and mutual funds—at least, that is what they tell their clients.

Or, if they admit they can't time the market and pick stocks, they tell their clients they can put the client's money with a money manager who can do these things.

But there is little independent, peer-reviewed, scientifically valid

MARKET TIMING refers to the supposed ability to forecast whether the market is at a peak or in a valley, and to profit from that prediction.

STOCK PICKING refers to the supposed ability to select stocks that are undervalued and will outperform the market over some future period of time.

evidence that anyone can successfully engage in either market timing or stock picking consistently over the long term. In fact, all the evidence concludes that the opposite is true. To be sure, every year some managers do "beat the market" by beating their benchmark index. A few managers even do it for many years in a row. But the number of managers who beat the market is the amount one would expect, given statistical chance. The fact that they beat the market is not proof that they are better at what they do than others. They beat the market due to simple statistical rules.

Financial consultants, money managers and mutual fund managers who attempt to beat the market are engaged in what I call "hyperactive management." And I call these investment professionals "hyperactive brokers and advisors" because that is what they are.

Smart-money investors avoid those advisors and money managers. They invest directly with fund managers who know that, absent a lucky streak, the market return is really the best return.

You should invest this way, too—for market returns.

If you ignore this advice, you are doing yourself a huge disservice. The **securities industry** adds costs. It subtracts value. Advisors who counsel their clients that they can beat the markets are assured of success in one area: transferring money from their clients' pockets to their own.

WHY HYPERACTIVE MANAGEMENT IS SO EXPENSIVE

The biggest problem with hyperactive management is expenses. They are so substantial that, when coupled with taxes and other hidden

---

The **SECURITIES INDUSTRY** is made up of the brokerage firms, investment banks, insurance companies, and other entities that develop, package and market stocks and bonds in order for corporations and government entities to raise capital from outside investors and for investors to seek investment returns.

---

costs, the odds against a hyperactively managed portfolio beating the comparable market returns over an extended period are very, very long.

The success of hyperactive brokers and advisors is really not success in investing, but *success in selling*. Their success in selling is based on five sacred beliefs, all of which are untrue:

1. Hyperactive brokers and advisors can beat the markets;
2. Hyperactive brokers and advisors can time the markets;
3. Market timing and stock selection are really important;
4. The more expensive a product or service, the more valuable it must be;
5. Things that are exclusive or elitist are more valuable.

It is a system that depends on its ability to convince you, through the expenditure of hundreds of millions of dollars of advertising, that you need to listen to these "experts." You don't. Smart Investors don't give their money to hyperactive brokers or advisers to do things that they can do better themselves.

3

Smart Investing Takes Less Time than Brunch

The first key to wisdom is defined, of course, as assiduous and frequent questioning.

—Pierre Abélard, 1079–1142, *Sic et Non*, translated by W. J. Lewis

So why is this the smartest investment book you'll ever read? Because it is simple. It is understandable. It doesn't beat around the bush and it doesn't pull punches. It tells you exactly why you should call your stock-picking, market-timing, stockbroker or investment advisor today and tell him or her you are taking control of your money.

You are moving your money where you can get superior long-term returns without the hassle and worry you currently have with your investments. You have seen the light—the light of investing for market returns.

If that isn't smart, I don't know what is.

Brokers and investment advisors cannot beat market returns over the long term.

They talk the talk, but they can't walk the walk.

There are hundreds of academic studies that demonstrate this fact conclusively.

If investors knew this, they wouldn't use these brokers or advisors. But the securities industry, assisted by the financial media, perpetuates the myth that they are able to beat the markets consistently over the long term, and they hide the data that demonstrate conclusively that this simply is not true.

Investors of all stripes lose billions of dollars a year because they don't understand that there is an easy, sure-fire way to achieve market returns without using brokers or investment advisors.

And achieving market returns is a big deal. That's because there is ample data indicating that, over the long term, simply achieving market returns will beat 95 percent of all professionally managed investment portfolios.

Now that I have told you this secret, I am going to explain how you can achieve market returns. It is simple, easy and not expensive.

It should not take you very long to read this book. But it is an investment of time that can change your life.

Once you have read the book, it shouldn't take you more than ninety minutes to fill out the necessary forms to have your money managed in a smart way. And after that, it shouldn't take you more than ninety minutes a year to make sure your investment portfolio continues to be structured the way you want it to be.

And you can do this yourself—you won't have to pay a broker or advisor.

Now, if taking control of your financial life in ninety minutes a year isn't smart, I don't know what is.

4

Drop Me to the Bottom Line!

More often (alas), the conclusions (supporting active management)
can only be justified by assuming that the laws of arithmetic have
been suspended for the convenience of those who choose to pursue
careers as active managers.

—William F. Sharpe, Nobel Laureate in Economics, 1990.
"The Arithmetic of Active Management," *Financial Analysts' Journal*,
Vol. 47, No. 1, January/February 1991

The chart on page 12 is the bottom line. When you look at it, keep in mind that the "Low Risk" portfolio has the highest percentage of **bonds** and the "High Risk" Portfolio has the highest percentage of **stocks**.

In less than a minute, you will understand the long-term historical returns and risks of the four portfolios that are suitable for the vast majority of investors. You can quickly compare the differences in returns and the differences in risk.

The chart on page 13 tells you the name of the funds and the correct percentage of those funds, in this example available from the Vanguard Group, that you should purchase for the portfolio you determine is the right one for you. Comparable information is provided in chapter 39 for funds available from other well-known fund families and for using Exchange Traded Funds.

It does not matter which of the fund families noted in chapter 38 you use because they all offer **index funds** with low initial investments and low annual charges. By "index fund," I mean a fund that holds all of the stocks in a specific segment of the market. For example, an S&P 500 index fund holds the stocks of the 500 widely held companies that make up that index. In this way, without trying to time the **market** or pick a stock winner, this type of fund will *always match the returns of the stocks of those 500 companies,* less the costs incurred by the fund.

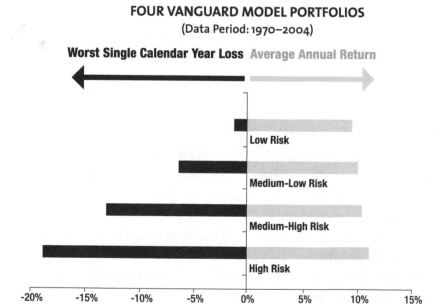

FOUR VANGUARD MODEL PORTFOLIOS
(Data Period: 1970–2004)

COMPOSITION OF FOUR VANGUARD MODEL PORTFOLIOS

FUND NAME	LOW RISK	MEDIUM-LOW RISK	MEDIUM-HIGH RISK	HIGH RISK
Total Stock Market Index Fund *(VTSMX)*	14%	28%	42%	56%
Total International Stock Index Fund *(VGTSX)*	6%	12%	18%	24%
Total Bond Market Index Fund *(VBMFX)*	80%	60%	40%	20%
	100%	100%	100%	100%

The overwhelming academic data indicates that investors who follow this advice will beat the returns of 95 percent or more of actively managed mutual funds over the long term.

No broker. No advisor.

No worry. No stress.

But I know you don't believe me. It just can't be this easy. You may even be skeptical about some of the data I discuss in this book. You can check the sources for all data by reading chapter 44.

All I ask is that you read on with an open mind.

A **MARKET** is a mechanism by which potential buyers and potential sellers of items can be matched. In the world of stock and bond investments, some markets are physical while others exist only as computer-to-computer interchanges.

STOCKS are ownership interests (equity) in companies. After a company has paid all of its expenses for the year (including taxes and interest on debt), the remainder belongs to the owners. The total money left divided by the number of shares of stock outstanding is known as the earnings per share (EPS). This EPS can be reused by the company for growth or can be returned to stockholders either as dividends or through a repurchase of the stock by the company. The price of a share of stock increases or decreases in relation to the value potential investors put on it when they analyze the company's prospects for continuing to earn more than the company's costs in the future.

BONDS are debt instruments. When you buy a bond you are lending money to a corporation or a government entity. You receive a steady interest payment in return for as long as you hold the bond. If you hold the bond to maturity, you receive the face value of the bond at the expiration. If you sell the bond in the open market, it may be worth more or less than face value, depending on the current interest rate of comparable bonds.

INDEX FUNDS are mutual funds (pools of money from many small investors) that invest in all or substantially all of the stocks or bonds that comprise a particular index, in their appropriate weighting. Index funds are often referred to as "passive investments" because their managers do not buy and sell securities in an effort to earn more than the return on the index.

5

Smart Investing Simply Makes Sense

If there are 10,000 people looking at the stocks and trying to pick winners, one in 10,000 is going to score, by chance alone, a great coup, and that's all that's going on. It's a game, it's a chance operation, and people think they are doing something purposeful . . . but they're really not.

—Merton Miller, Nobel Laureate in Economics.
Transcript of the PBS *Nova* special "The Trillion-Dollar Bet," 2000

When President Bush and Republican congressional leaders decided to try to eliminate the estate tax, they did a very smart thing. They took the advice of some scholars at a conservative think tank and started referring to the estate tax as the "death tax."

Public perception of this tax immediately changed. Today, you can spend an hour explaining to a middle- or low-income person how there is absolutely no way his or her estate will have to pay any estate tax, and that person will probably still vote for a politician who says he wants to eliminate the death tax.

Such is the power of a name.

Those of us who advise clients on how to invest for market returns find ourselves in a similar situation as those who for years have wanted to eliminate the estate tax. The current terminology is a snore; it makes our readers' and our clients' eyes glaze over.

The current terminology for investing for market returns is "passive investing." What could be more boring? Do you want to be an active investor or a passive investor? No one wants to be passive; it implies that you have no ability to have any influence on an outcome.

Another term historically used for market-return investing is "index-based investing"—another less-than-scintillating bit of verbiage.

Over the years, index-based or passive investing has come to be equated with being "average." And no one wants to be average. We all want to live in Garrison Keillor's Lake Wobegone, where all the women are strong, all the men are good-looking and all the children are above average.

That's why we listen to hyperactive brokers and advisors who say, "Why do you want your portfolio to be average? I can help you make your portfolio superior. Our analysts can find undervalued stocks for you. We can determine when the market is overbought or oversold and help you manage your portfolio to go into and out of the market to maximize your return." Sound familiar?

But in reality, there is nothing passive or average about investing for market returns. Nothing could be farther from the truth. This nomenclature is outdated and unfortunate, and it needs to be abandoned.

Welcome to the new world of "Smart Investing." It is populated by "Smart Investors."

You should be a Smart Investor.

Smart Investing is very simple. In a Smart Investment portfolio, you hold investments in a group of funds that, in turn, have investments in all the securities (stocks or bonds) in a particular index. This portfolio is very easy to implement.

You will hold investments in funds that represent three broad indexes. The three types of index funds you will hold are:

1. An index fund representative of the United States stock market in its broadest terms;
2. An index fund representative of the international stock market in its broadest terms; and
3. An index fund representative of the United States bond market in its broadest terms.

I will show you how to determine the exact percentage of your portfolio that you will hold in each of these three types of index funds in greater detail later, and will give you the names of the index funds in which you should invest.

Smart Investing is, in reality, extremely aggressive, intelligent and very rewarding. It is based on academically verifiable data and quantitative risk management.

This data shows clearly and unmistakably that, over the long term, Smart Investors will consistently outperform those who attempt to beat the markets. That's not average; that's superior.

Conversely, investing with the goal of beating the markets is an ill-defined art, not a science. It is characterized by a lack of risk measurement. It is akin to financial astrology. It is, in many ways, the equivalent to gambling at a casino.

I call that approach "Hyperactive Investing." "Hyperactive Investors" listen to brokers and other financial advisors spin their tales of how one particular stock or another will somehow defy the logic of market efficiency, how the whole world is wrong but that broker is right and the stock is not currently priced correctly. If you truly believe in markets, you believe that the market does, by definition, price each and every stock correctly as determined by buyers willing to buy at any given price and sellers willing to sell at any given price.

It is an easy choice: Smart Investing based on reams of sound academic data that is easily verifiable, or Hyperactive Investing, based on hype and hope?

You may be surprised to learn that, according to a recent study, Smart Investing accounts for the vast majority of the trades in the United States. Unfortunately, it is likely that you, your friends and neighbors are part of the disadvantaged minority if you are relying on the advice of your hyperactive broker or advisor.

It's time to become a Smart Investor.

PART TWO

YOUR BROKER OR ADVISOR IS KEEPING YOU FROM BEING A SMART INVESTOR

6

Brokers Make Money When They Are Hyperactive

Q: "So investors shouldn't delude themselves about beating the market?"

A: "They're just not going to do it. It's just not going to happen."

—Daniel Kahneman, Nobel Laureate in Economics, 2002.
Interview reported in the *Orange County Register*, Jan. 2, 2002

Virtually all actively managed funds have, as a goal, beating a **"benchmark index."** For example many funds have, as their "benchmark index," the goal of beating an index consisting of all of the stocks that make up the S&P 500.

Clearly, these funds provide no value to investors—or even a negative value—if they cannot beat their designated indexes, because investors could assure themselves of achieving the returns of the index—every year—by simply investing in an index fund that holds all of the stocks in that index.

Therefore, it is of great significance (and a deep, dark secret rarely discussed by hyperactive brokers and advisors), that in excess of 90

> A **BENCHMARK INDEX** is an index that mutual funds use to compare their investment performance against. The best-known benchmark index is the Standard and Poor's 500, the index of 500 of the largest American companies by market capitalization. Mutual funds that invest in U.S. large-capitalization stocks typically use the S&P 500 Index as their benchmark.

percent of actively managed mutual funds *fail* to equal or beat their benchmark indexes over the long term.

Indeed, you can look at any meaningful time period and you will find that the majority of hyperactively managed funds fail to beat an unmanaged S&P 500 index, even when it is their stated goal to do so.

Study after study shows that, over a long period, Smart Investors outperform Hyperactive Investors. Smart Investors should continue to outperform the vast majority of Hyperactive Investors who attempt to beat the markets by either trading themselves or using hyperactive brokers or advisors.

Hyperactive Investors lead the pack in one category: stress. They are on a fool's errand and don't know it. They believe they must constantly monitor the markets and listen to the conflicting views of the financial pundits. When all this attention still results in underperformance or even cataclysmic losses, their stress level goes off the charts.

The reason for the dismal record of Hyperactive Investors is a combination of trading costs and management fees. Hyperactive funds cost more (average fees of 1.5 percent per year vs. fees of under 0.35 percent for most index funds) and trade more. Trading increases costs. Increased costs, through fees and trading costs, makes it exceedingly difficult for hyperactively managed funds to equal the performance of index funds and that is why most of them fail to do so.

Here is what the raw data tells us:

- Hyperactively managed funds significantly underperform the market over the long term.

- It is much less stressful to be a Smart Investor.
- It is much less expensive to be a Smart Investor.
- Most investors do not need any broker or advisor to be a Smart Investor.

Here is the bottom line: Smart Investors will fare significantly better over the long run than Hyperactive Investors.

7

A Loser's Game

Even as Wall Street belittles your investment abilities, it also wants you to believe you can beat the stock-market averages. This, of course, is contradictory. But it is also entirely self-serving. The more you trade and the more you invest with active money managers, the more money the Street makes. Increasingly, some of the market's savviest investors have turned their back on this claptrap. They have given up on active managers who pursue market-beating returns and instead have bought market-tracking index funds. But Wall Street doesn't want you to buy index funds, because they aren't a particularly profitable product for the Street. Instead, Wall Street wants you to keep shooting for market-beating returns. That is why you should be suspicious when you hear talk of the supposed "stock picker's market."

—Jonathan Clements, author of *You've Lost It, Now What?*

The actual returns of Hyperactive Investors are even worse than you might think.

One telling study demonstrated that the average hyperactively managed fund investor had an annualized return for the twenty-year period from 1985 to 2004 of 3.7 percent, when the S&P 500 index returned 13.2 percent. The investor would have done better with bank certificates of deposit!

Another study examined the actual shareholder returns in specific actively managed funds and compared them to the reported returns of those funds. In fund after fund, Hyperactive Investors significantly underperformed the reported returns. For example, for the period 1998 to 2001, the Fidelity Aggressive Growth Fund reported returns of 2.8 percent, but the average Hyperactive Investor in that fund had a *loss* of 24.1 percent.

If the average fund earned 13.2 percent, shouldn't the average investor in those funds also have earned 13.2 percent? She should, but she doesn't. That's because Hyperactive Investors chase hot-performing funds. These investors pour their money into mutual funds *after* periods of good performance, hoping for a repeat performance. They are often disappointed.

Stated differently, Hyperactive Investors buy and sell stocks and/or mutual funds frequently.

I ask you, what could be sillier than frequently buying and selling mutual funds?

Mutual funds were originally conceived on the idea that small investors should not be buying and selling individual stocks frequently because transaction costs would eat up any potential profit. Instead, small investors should pool their money into a mutual fund, where a "professional" money manager buys and sells the stocks for them, in large blocks, with much lower commissions than an individual investor could get. In this way, the investor can "buy and hold" a good mutual fund and the fund manager can indulge his or her illusive goal of beating the markets through stock picking and market timing.

Nice theory.

But today, hyperactive brokers and advisors often recommend that their clients sell old mutual funds and invest in the next "hot" fund. This way, these "investment professionals" can continue to generate sales commissions.

Remember this: The proof is overwhelming that Smart Investing—investing for market returns—outperforms attempting to beat the markets over the long term.

Why then is it so difficult to convince individual investors to be Smart Investors? There are a number of reasons, but the most compelling has to do with a marketing juggernaut of hyperactive brokers—paid for with money earned from their clients, no less.

Another equally important reason has to do with human psychology.

And yet a third has to do with what is called "financial pornography," the incessant blathering of financial writers and talking heads from the print press, television, the Web and other media sources.

By the way, I know your time is valuable. So if at any time you feel convinced and don't want to read any more, you can skip right to chapter 36, where I lay out a four-step process for taking control of your financial life and becoming a Smart Investor.

8

Why Investors Pursue Hyperactive Investing

Santa Claus and the Easter Bunny should take a few pointers from the mutual-fund industry [and its fund managers]. All three are trying to pull off elaborate hoaxes. But while Santa and the bunny suffer the derision of eight-year-olds everywhere, actively managed stock funds still have an ardent following among otherwise clear-thinking adults. This continued loyalty amazes me. Reams of statistics prove that most of the fund industry's stock pickers fail to beat the market. For instance, over the 10 years through 2001, U.S. stock funds returned 12.4% a year, vs. 12.9% for the Standard & Poor's 500 stock index.

—Jonathan Clements, "Only Fools Fall in . . . Managed Funds?"
Wall Street Journal, September 15, 2002

The evidence that Smart Investing is superior to Hyperactive Investing is both compelling and overwhelming. Yet in excess of 90 percent of all *individual* investors continue to be Hyperactive Investors.

Here are the primary reasons.

MARKETING

Hyperactive brokers and advisors spend hundreds of millions of dollars on very slick marketing campaigns to push their services. Who can forget the television commercial where the broker assumes the role of father of the bride? Those of us who are old enough still remember John Houseman, the wonderful actor who played the law school professor in *The Paper Chase*, telling us that the company he represented "make(s) money the old-fashioned way, we earn it." And who doesn't remember the name of the brokerage firm for which everybody in the ad stops to listen when the broker from that firm whispers into his client's ear?

Guess where all the money comes from for these companies to create those marketing campaigns and buy those advertising pages and minutes? Of course: It comes from the commissions and other fees charged to those hapless Hyperactive Investors with the supposedly invaluable assistance of their Hyperactive Advisors.

How perfect is that? The firms that separate you from your money use a piece of that money to create more marketing and advertising material to get you and others to give them more money to invest—at lower returns than you can get from being a Smart Investor.

Kind of like digging your own grave before the firing squad mows you down.

GAMBLING

There is a well-documented psychological attraction to gambling activities; we all have this attraction to one degree or another. Some people indulge in "recreational" gambling at a casino. Others have a more profound attraction and gamble more frequently and for larger stakes than others.

Being a Hyperactive Investor fuels this psychological attraction. The fact that Hyperactive Brokers and Advisors can produce intermittent "winners" reinforces this instinct, just like the sound of coins hitting the tray at a slot machine. But just as gamblers ultimately fall to the house at the casino, Hyperactive Investors will ultimately be the losers. The house in this case is the brokerage firm.

DESIRE TO SEEK ORDER

There is another well-documented human tendency—to find order where it does not exist, and thus to confuse luck with skill. The most commonly cited example is research that found a basketball player with a "hot hand" is no more likely to make his next shot than at any other time. Shooting a basketball is essentially like tossing a coin. Every shot is an independent event, and the chances of making it have to do more with how close the player is to the basket and how much pressure he or she is under than whether or not the player has made the last six shots.

In the financial world, the widespread use of so-called technical tools to predict the market is a perfect example of this desire for order. Technical analysis, which uses these technical tools, looks at patterns of stock prices (so-called charting) in an effort to divine the stock's next movement. There are exhaustive studies demonstrating that technical analysis has absolutely no validity, yet it continues to be used by many Hyperactive Investors and their brokers.

OVERCONFIDENCE

People are overconfident in their own abilities. This is particularly true of men, whose perception of their skills in many areas—especially athletics—is often at odds with objective reality.

The vast majority of hyperactive brokers and advisors underperform the markets over the long term. Few will admit it and most retain total confidence in their ability to beat the markets in the future. Or at least they appear to have this confidence, which is a very good sales tool.

Really, if your hyperactive broker or advisor told you the truth and said, "I have no idea where the markets are headed or which stocks are a good buy," would you use his or her services?

LOOKING FOR "SIZZLE" (IN ALL THE WRONG PLACES)

A financial pundit recently noted that convincing people to invest for market returns has the same appeal as serving a vegetarian dinner at a cattlemens' convention. There is no "sizzle." No "double your money in six weeks." No complicated software to learn. No "hot" stock or mutual fund to select.

There is no rush that Hyperactive Investors get from that feeling of dealing with their hyperactive brokers on a constant basis and trying to outwit other investors. No bragging rights at the nineteenth hole as to what a great broker they have and how their broker picked a stock that "really took off." No need to even follow the financial pundits, much less engage in the kind of frenetic, counterproductive and obsessive attention to every new scrap of financial news generated by media, delivered breathlessly, minute by minute, throughout the day.

Understanding the reasons why investors ignore reality and continue to be Hyperactive Investors is very important.

It is significant that superior market performance is not one of them. To the contrary, Smart Investors have demonstrably superior returns over the long term.

You would think that this fact would carry the day.

9

The "Activity" Myth

Properly measured, the average actively managed dollar must underperform the average passively managed dollar, net of costs.

—William F. Sharpe, Nobel Laureate in Economics, 1990.

"The Arithmetic of Active Management," *Financial Analysts Journal*,

Vol. 47, No. 1, January/February 1991

Most people confuse activity with progress and passivity with lack of initiative. That is part of the problem with the current investing nomenclature.

With investing, activity is not progress. Activity is cost. And cost just eats up investment return.

A well-known study demonstrated that investors who engage in the most trading are the ones who most significantly underperform the market. The conclusion of the study was that ". . . trading is hazardous to your wealth."

Hyperactive brokers and advisors, and especially online firms for do-it-yourself investors, encourage trading. They tell investors to sell stocks or funds that have underperformed in order to "get rid of dogs" and use the tax loss to offset gains on other trades. They encourage investors to buy the next "hot" stock or fund.

But study after study shows that all of this trading does only one thing for investors—it transfers money from their accounts to their hyperactive brokers' and advisors' pockets in the form of commissions and fees.

That is a major reason why Smart Investors generally fare better than Hyperactive Investors.

10

What's Wrong with Hyperactive Investing?

Why does indexing outmaneuver the best minds on Wall Street? Paradoxically, it is because the best and brightest in the financial community have made the stock market very efficient. When information arises about individual stocks or the market as a whole, it gets reflected in stock prices without delay, making one stock as reasonably priced as another. Active managers who frequently shift from security to security actually detract from performance [compared to an index fund] by incurring transaction costs.

—Burton G. Malkiel, "Why The Critics Are Wrong,"
Wall Street Journal Interactive Edition, May 24, 1999

What is wrong with trying to beat the markets?

Just about everything.

The corporate culture is troublesome. And many, if not most, of the Hyperactive Brokers and Advisors who encourage their clients to be Hyperactive Investors are qualified only in sales, not in finance.

But the biggest reason is that the Wall Street investing approach is premised on a set of beliefs that have *no* credible support:

- Hyperactive brokers and advisors can time the market;
- Hyperactive brokers and advisors can pick stocks or mutual funds that will "beat the market."
- Hyperactive brokers and advisors can pick fund managers who will "beat the market."

In addition:

- The system ignores the effects of fees, trading costs and other expenses, taxes and inflation, on the ultimate investment returns.
- The system is fraught with conflicts of interest, from broker compensation to the relationship between advertising and news in the financial media.
- The system often fails to measure risk, thereby exposing investors to portfolios that are far too risky, with terrible consequences.
- The system has successfully avoided being held to a fiduciary standard because it knows that it cannot meet that standard in its relationships with investors.
- The system imposes a biased and unfair "mandatory arbitration" process on investors who invest within it. Investors who have been victimized by broker misconduct are frequently victimized again when they are forced to use this industry-run, dispute resolution forum to recover their losses.

In short, being a Hyperactive Investor is a fool's errand. It is a zero-sum game (or worse, when you consider transaction costs), except for the hyperactive brokers and advisors who encourage you to do so.

They make out just fine.

11

Brokers Aren't on Your Side

It [is] a fundamental dishonesty, a fundamental problem that cuts to
the core of the lack of integrity on Wall Street.

—Eliot L. Spitzer, Attorney General of New York,

interviewed for *NOW with Bill Moyers*

You need to have utmost trust, faith and confidence in your financial advisor and in the firm that employs him or her.

But there is unsettling news about their integrity—or lack thereof. One study looked at the analyst ratings of fifty banking and brokerage firms as they related to nineteen companies that went bankrupt in 2002. The study demonstrated that:

1. Forty-seven of the fifty firms continued to advise investors to buy or hold shares in the companies up to the date the companies filed for bankruptcy.
2. Twelve of the nineteen companies continued to receive "buy" or "hold" ratings on the actual date they filed for bankruptcy.

In 2002 many of the best known and most well-respected brokerage firms, which employ hoards of hyperactive brokers, entered into a $1.4 billion settlement (without admitting that they had done anything wrong!) to resolve allegations that they duped their clients (you, your friends and your neighbors) by issuing misleading analyst reports.

If prominent brokerage firms filled with hyperactive brokers have no demonstrated ability to give accurate and reliable advice, and if you give credence to New York Attorney General Eliot Spitzer's observation about their "lack of integrity," why would you continue to rely on them for investment advice?

No advisor who advocates Smart Investing was the subject of any of these allegations. These advisors do not believe, employ or rely upon stock analysts.

Smart Investing advisors make no predictions about the future performance of the market as a whole or about any particular stock. Instead, they focus on **asset classes** (and their returns), **asset allocation**, and **risk management** and a solid, academically based belief system that has consistently been demonstrated to outperform hyperactive brokers and advisors over the long term.

Make proper asset allocation your new investment goal. Once you accept the premise that asset allocation is far more important than stock picking or market timing, your financial life becomes a stress-free walk in the park and your money will start to grow.

ASSET CLASSES are the three major groupings under which financial assets fall: stocks, bonds and cash. Stocks are ownership shares in a company. Bonds are loans to a company or a government entity. Cash is not just currency, but also checking and savings accounts held in banks and money market funds.

ASSET ALLOCATION is the way that asset classes are divided up in an investment portfolio. Depending on an individual investor's time horizon and tolerance for risk, he or she will allocate the money in the portfolio in different proportions among stocks, bonds and cash.

RISK MANAGEMENT refers to the techniques that can be used to reduce the risk in an investment portfolio. Risk is the measure of the probability of potential outcomes and the change in portfolio value that would occur if those outcomes came to pass.

12

Hyperactive Brokers, Underachieving Students

Training for a new broker goes something like this: study and take the Series 7, 63, 65 and insurance exams. I spent three weeks in classes learning about products, mutual funds, and learning to sell. If a broker wants to learn about [asset allocation and diversification] it has to be done on the broker's own time.

—Anonymous former broker, major Wall Street firm, quoted in Daniel R. Solin, *Does Your Broker Owe You Money?*

Call me picky, but if I am going to entrust my life savings to an advisor (assuming that I need one at all; most Smart Investors don't), I want him or her to have a Ph.D. in finance, or comparable credentials, from a major university. After all, isn't knowledge of finance the critical skill needed to give investment advice?

I don't have much regard for the credentials bandied about by hyperactive brokers and financial advisors. Titles like "Vice President, Investments" are handed out like candy, and not on the basis of academic credentials, client service or even the performance of their clients' portfolios. They are handed out on the basis of commissions and fees generated for the firm.

I wouldn't use any advisor, regardless of his or her qualifications, who tells me that he or she can beat the markets, but it is good to know something about real qualifications anyway.

Only a small percentage of hyperactive brokers and advisors have credentials indicating that they have engaged in any serious study of finance. As I will explain later, the vast majority of Smart Investors do not need to spend money on *any* advisor. Instead, they should invest the money they would otherwise be paying an advisor in order to increase their total nest egg.

13

What Do You Think of These Odds?

[S]kepticism about past returns is crucial. The truth is, much as you may wish you could know which funds will be hot, you can't—and neither can the legions of advisors and publications that claim they can.

—Bethany McLean, "The Skeptic's Guide to Mutual Funds,"
Fortune, March 15, 1999

The next three chapters have to do with the inability of hyperactive brokers, advisors and investment managers to time the market or pick winners. Before that, I want to tell you about a study done by my colleague and friend Edward S. O'Neal, Ph.D., an assistant professor of finance at the Babcock Graduate School of Management at Wake Forest University, which was published in my previous book, *Does Your Broker Owe You Money?* As I have stated, there are many academic studies that show that Hyperactive Investing is a fool's errand. I like Professor O'Neal's study because it is so easy to understand.

First he looked at the performance of all 494 actively managed mutual funds that had, as their goal, beating the S&P 500 index for the five-year period July 1993 through June 1998.

How hard could this be? The managers of these funds are among the best, brightest and highest-paid people in this country. Some of them earn millions of dollars to beat the S&P 500. Their funds charge more than eight times the charge of a simple index fund, like the Vanguard 500 Index Fund (VFINX). And we know the Vanguard 500 Index Fund will *always* give investors the returns of the S&P 500 index (reduced only by the amount of its low fees), because it is set up to do precisely that.

O'Neal then did the same analysis for the next five-year period, from July 1998 through June 2003.

Here is what he found: Only 46 percent of the actively managed funds beat the index during the first five-year period, and only a pathetic 8 percent beat the index during the second five-year period.

And here is the real kicker. How many of these funds beat the S&P 500 index during *both* periods? In Professor O'Neal's own words:

> These results are sad indeed. The number of funds that beat the market in both periods is a whopping 10—or only 2 percent of all large cap funds.

Here is Professor O'Neal's bottom line. It should be yours as well:

> Investors, both individual and institutional, and particularly 401(k) plans, would be far better served by investing in passive or passively managed funds than in trying to pick more expensive active managers who purport to be able to beat the markets.

Professor O'Neal's study also demonstrates that there is no relationship between a fund that performs well during one period and its performance during an ensuing period. This irrefutable fact makes the exercise of trying to pick a "winning" fund even more improbable.

Of course, you could try to be one of the lucky investors who picks one of the 2 percent of funds that beat the markets. Or you could confront statistical reality and common sense and invest in an index fund that will give you market returns 100 percent of the time.

The choice seems obvious, but most investors, egged on by their hyperactive brokers and advisors, make the wrong one. They attempt to find a "hot" fund that will "beat" the markets, and suffer the inevitable costly consequences. Smart Investors don't chase "hot" funds.

14

Nobody Can Time
the Market

If I have noticed anything over these 60 years on Wall Street, it is
that people do not succeed in forecasting what's going to happen to
the stock market.

—Benjamin Graham, coauthor of *Security Analysis*

I f anyone could consistently time the market, you would think it
would be the authors of market-timing newsletters. They charge investors for access to their tip sheets about when to move money into
or out of particular markets. But a study of more than 15,000 predictions made by 237 market-timing newsletters between June 1980 and
December 1992 demonstrated that 94.5 percent of the newsletters had
gone out of business, with an average length of operations of about four
years.

What if your broker was Alan Greenspan, the venerable former
chairman of the Federal Reserve Board? How lucky you are! Who in
the world knows more about the direction of the markets than Alan
Greenspan?

Alan calls you. He says he is worried that the market is overheated. He refers to the investor enthusiasm for stocks as "irrational exuberance." He is concerned about a meltdown similar to the one experienced in Japan in the early 1990s.

Would you listen to him and dump the stocks in your portfolio? I suspect you would.

Well, Alan made such a prediction, in 1996. And if you had listened to him you would have missed out on a three-year stock-market boom where the S&P 500 doubled in value.

So much for Mr. Greenspan's ability to time the market.

Do you think your hyperactive broker or advisor has more reliable information than Alan Greenspan?

The reason neither Alan Greenspan nor your hyperactive broker or advisor can accurately predict the financial markets is that neither of them has the power to change the psychology of these markets. Alan Greenspan's comment about "irrational exuberance" was his attempt to use his position of influence to "talk the market down" from the dizzying heights it had begun to attain even early in what we know now in hindsight was a bubble.

Although his remarks caused a little downward blip, there was enough energy in the market to propel it upward for more than another three years. Any prediction that a financial market will go up or that a financial market will go down is, at some point, going to prove right. The issue is when that time will be.

Those who adhere to market timing almost always miss the absolute top or the absolute bottom. They are either too early, like those who bailed out when Alan Greenspan first spoke of irrational exuberance. Or they are too late, like those who hung on through 2001 and 2002 after the stock market crashed and burned, because other stock-market "experts" told them to use "dips in the market [as] buying opportunities."

But creating the illusion of their ability to time the market is critical to the business of hyperactive brokers and advisors. After all, if they have this ability and you don't, you need to rely on their advice, which means you need to pay their fees. The only problem is that this is an expertise they don't have, because it is an expertise that does not exist.

Yet the talking heads on TV and many hyperactive brokers and advisors are always talking about what is going to happen in the market, as if they actually have information upon which to make these prognostications.

They don't.

No one does.

Market timing, like stock picking (which I'll discuss in a little while) is nothing but a shell game. You should never listen to anyone who says he or she can time the market, no matter how qualified or confident that person appears to be.

Advisors to Smart Investors never rely on market timing. They understand that if Alan Greenspan can't do it, neither can they.

Smart Investors never engage in market timing because they know it is a sham.

15

Nobody Can Consistently Beat the Market

The economists arrived at a devastating conclusion: It seemed just as plausible to attribute the success of top traders to sheer luck, rather than skill.

—From the PBS *Nova* special "The Trillion-Dollar Bet," Feb. 8, 2000

S tock picking" refers to the ability to select stocks or mutual funds that will outperform the market.

Virtually all hyperactive brokers and advisors tell you they have the ability to engage in stock picking. After all, that is how they justify the fat fees and commissions they get paid.

Every actively managed mutual fund manager believes he or she has this ability.

Here's a true story, not like the story about the chimp who performs open-heart surgery.

After I published my previous book, *Does Your Broker Owe You Money?*, I received telephone calls and e-mails from brokers and ex-brokers who told me stories that would make your skin crawl.

One of my favorites was told by a man who had left work with a major brokerage firm in order to advise clients to invest for market returns. He told me about the training he had received a few years earlier when he started work with a major—and well-respected—brokerage firm. He and the other brokers in training were told to split their potential client list in half. They were told to call half and tell them to buy a particular stock. The other half were to receive calls telling them to sell the same stock.

In two weeks, these "financial advisor" trainees were told to see which way the stock had moved, up or down. Whichever way it had moved, half of the potential client list would think the trainee was pretty smart, to be able to pick a stock like that.

They were told to split this "successful" half of their group again, and do the same thing: tell half that a stock would go up and half that the same stock would go down.

If they did this three times, and started with a call list of 120 potential clients, after three "successful stock picks" they should then have fifteen "warm leads," people who had enough confidence in their ability to pick stocks to become clients.

Talk about a shell game!

If anyone could successfully pick stocks, you would think it would be the much-touted analysts who work for the most prestigious Wall Street firms. After all, they spend all of their time studying companies, trying to glean information that will assist them in selecting stocks that will outperform the market. It is their work product that hyperactive brokers often use as the basis for recommendations to Hyperactive Investors.

However, many studies of analyst recommendations find little support for their ability to pick stock winners. These studies indicate that analysts are right sometimes and wrong sometimes. When analysts are wrong, it is the investors who rely on their supposed expertise who lose money.

For example, as one prominent study by Patrick Bajari and John Krainer noted: "[I]n 2000 and 2001, the least recommended stocks earned an average abnormal return of 13%, while the most highly recommended stocks earned average abnormal returns of –7%." Ouch!

Even studies that demonstrate that there can be value in analyst recommendations note that in order to take advantage of them, such heavy trading is required that these transaction costs essentially offset the benefits obtained by relying on these recommendations.

If this is true, it is difficult to understand what value these recommendations really have—even when they are correct.

Finally, given the number of analyst recommendations, and the conflicting studies about their reliability, how do Hyperactive Investors know which ones have value and which ones don't? It clearly is a crap shoot.

Unfortunately, as with market timing, there is no evidence that anyone can consistently engage in stock picking. And, as I'll explain later, it turns out that stock picking accounts for only a small minority of all of the trades in the U.S. markets, and that number is declining. Clearly, the message is getting out. Unfortunately, it has not reached the vast majority of individual investors or virtually all hyperactive brokers and advisors who give them "professional advice."

Smart Investors do not engage in stock picking. They know that it is a fool's errand.

Smart Investors are not fools.

16

Nobody Can Pick "Hot" Fund Managers

[T]o be fair, I don't think that you'd want to pay much attention to Morningstar's star ratings either.

—John Rekenthaler, director of research,
Morningstar, *In the Vanguard*, Autumn 2000

Morningstar gives this fund its five-star rating!"
How many times have you heard that line from your hyperactive broker who is trying to convince you to buy a "hot" mutual fund?

It is a convincing pitch. After all, Morningstar is the industry leader in ranking mutual funds, using its "star" system. It would be hard to find anyone who does not agree that Morningstar has more data about mutual funds than anyone else in the world. Most people think that, with these vast resources, Morningstar could predict mutual funds that would outperform the markets.

Most people are wrong.

Morningstar rates mutual funds by giving them from one to five stars depending on their performance. A five-star rating indicates the best performing funds. Although Morningstar notes that its ratings system should not be used to predict future performance, many hyperactive brokers and advisors ignore this admonition.

An exhaustive study of the performance record of funds rated "five stars" by Morningstar failed to find reliable statistical evidence that these funds performed any better than funds rated four stars or even three stars. The study also found that Morningstar ratings did only marginally better than other, far more simplistic, predictors of future performance.

So much for the predictive ability of the "star" system.

If Morningstar can't do it, ask yourself whether you should listen to your hyperactive broker or advisor who claims that he or she can. No one has the ability to predict the next "hot" manager. All we know is that it is unlikely that he or she will be "hot" for long.

Hyperactive Investors typically hold a mutual fund in their portfolio for four years or less.

Why do they switch funds? After all, as I previously noted, the concept of a mutual fund was to allow small investors who didn't have time to research investments and pick their own stocks to "buy and hold" a fund and let the "investment professional" do the stock picking.

Hyperactive Investors switch funds because they are convinced by the financial media or by their hyperactive broker or advisor that they can do better in a "hot" mutual fund run by a "hot" mutual fund manager. And the coveted Morningstar five-star rating is frequently what convinces these investors to sell lower-rated funds and buy the newly designated ones rated "five stars."

Why do some hyperactive brokers misuse the Morningstar rating system in this manner? More trading means more commissions.

Unfortunately, it also means lower returns.

Smart Investors don't care who is "hot" and who is not. And they place no more value on Morningstar's "star" ratings than they do on the movement of the planets.

17

Why Recommend This Mutual Fund?

"American Funds dressed up these arrangements with fancy names like 'execution revenue,' 'target commissions' or 'Broker Partnership Payments,'" said Lockyer. "But when you look beneath the cloak of legitimacy, the payments are little more than kickbacks to buy preferential treatment. Investors deserve to know that. The law American Funds violated is based on that simple principle."

—California Attorney General Bill Lockyer, commenting on a securities fraud lawsuit filed against American Funds' Los Angeles–based distributor and investment manager. Press release dated March 23, 2005

There are literally thousands of mutual funds. Hyperactive brokers and advisors make recommendations every day about which one you and other investors should buy.

Most people think that when a broker or financial advisor makes a mutual fund recommendation that the investor is receiving objective advice about funds that can beat the markets.

Of course, as we have seen, no one has the ability to select such funds with any consistency. But still, in any given year, a number of mutual funds do outperform their benchmark index.

A **PROSPECTUS** is a document that should be given to a potential investor before he or she makes an investment. Every mutual fund has a prospectus, as does an initial public offering of stock. The prospectus defines the risks of the potential investment, as well as the investment philosophy and the capitalization of the stock or mutual fund the investor is being solicited to invest in.

So how does a broker decide what particular fund to recommend to Hyperactive Investors?

As with most other things within the financial services system, the recommendation decision is often driven by money.

Brokerage firms and brokers, and some independent advisors, are also paid a commission by the fund distributor when they sell a particular mutual fund.

Brokerage firms are paid for "shelf space" so they will recommend some mutual funds and not others. Charles Schwab, the founder of one of the largest discount brokerage firms, used the metaphor of the financial supermarket to try to get investors to understand that they could come to Schwab and buy any mutual fund, from any "brand" or fund family. And just like supermarkets, Schwab and other brokerage firms started charging mutual fund managers for preferential treatment.

This preferential treatment goes both ways—sometimes brokerage firms that sell enough mutual fund shares to their retail customers are also given favorable treatment by the mutual fund manager, who trades shares in the stocks that are bought and sold for the mutual fund through the brokerage firm's institutional brokerage arm.

If you read the fine print of any mutual fund **prospectus**, these fees are disclosed. But you really have to be a diligent reader.

I have never met an investor who realized that the brokerage firm he or she deals with regularly receives a financial inducement (to use a euphemistic term for this practice—some, like the Attorneys General of New York and California have gone so far as to call it a kickback) to make mutual fund recommendations.

It is bad enough that there is no evidence to support a hyperactive broker's claims about his or her ability to select mutual funds that will beat the market. It is worse that his or her recommendation is influenced by these payments.

If you needed another reason not to use hyperactive brokers or advisors, this is a good one to adopt. Smart Investors use advisors who do not receive fees from anyone other than their clients. Their advice is totally objective.

18

Hyperactive Investing Is Expensive

Investing is a strange business. It's the only one we know of where the more expensive the products get, the more customers want to buy them.

—Anthony M. Gallea and William Patalon III, coauthors of *Contrarian Investing*

Why pay more to achieve less? The costs imposed on the clueless Hyperactive Investors are one of the major reasons why they fare so poorly.

The stated "expense ratio" of the average hyperactive mutual fund (the cost of running the fund, a cost borne by the fund's investors) is 1.58 percent of the fund's total assets. This is the cost of salaries and other compensation (which is often high), utilities, computers and telecommunications, research services and explicit marketing costs such as glossy brochures and lunch for retail brokers when the mutual fund "wholesaler" goes to visit and pitch his or her wares.

When the other hidden, but very real, costs are added (such as trading commissions and payments for preferential treatment) this cost increases to 2.5 percent. Think about that for a moment. If, in a given year, the relevant benchmark for this fund returns 10 percent, a hyperactive fund that is trying to "beat the market" would have to return more than 12.5 percent in order to achieve this goal. And these costs do not include taxes, which are paid by the investor depending on his or her tax circumstances and can significantly reduce the investor's net return on the average mutual fund investment.

The average cost of funds that seek market returns is less than 0.2 percent. The typical advisor who seeks only market returns usually charges an annual fee of about 1 percent on the first $1 million in the portfolio, and less than 1 percent for greater amounts.

Since most Smart Investors do not need any advisor, their expenses can generally be kept to about 0.5 percent (or less), a savings of about 2 percent on investments in hyperactively managed funds. On a $100,000 investment, that is $2,000 *per year* in the Smart Investor's pocket rather than in the mutual fund company's profit line or in the coffers of the hyperactive brokerage firm.

And the taxes paid on investments in funds seeking market returns are a fraction of those incurred by hyperactive funds. This is because limited trading is performed by these funds. They only buy or sell shares in a stock when that company comes into or falls out of the particular index they are matching.

The difference between the internal costs of hyperactive funds and those invested for market returns is a primary reason why you should become a Smart Investor. Market return funds have such a significant cost advantage that they are likely to outperform hyperactive funds by approximately the difference in these fund management costs.

Have I convinced you yet? If so, you can skip right to chapter 36, which describes the four-step process for achieving vastly superior market returns.

In this case, you don't get what you pay for. The *less* expensive product is the superior one.

I know this is counterintuitive, but when you understand the relationship between low transaction costs, lower taxes (due to significantly less trading) and superior fund performance, you are well on your way to understanding why you have a responsibility, for your sake and for the financial security of your loved ones, to become a Smart Investor.

19

If It Walks Like a Duck and Quacks Like a Duck...

But before you jump [into managed accounts], consider the cost: typically, 2 percent to 3 percent of your assets per year. That sounds like pocket change in a year you earn 20 percent. But it's up to one-third of your stock profits in an average year, and two-thirds of the average profits in bonds. You are simply giving your money away. "It's one of the great marketing gimmicks," said Eli Neusner of Cerulli Associates, a Boston-based consulting firm.

—Jane Bryant Quinn, WashingtonPost.com, May 19, 1996

It probably is a duck.

Since the late 1990s, brokerage firms have become very successful in convincing Hyperactive Investors to pay an annual management fee—a so-called wrap fee—instead of a commission on fund or stock purchases. These firms frequently charge 2 percent or even 3 percent of the portfolio's value as a wrap fee.

The wrap account first appeared in the mid 1990s in an effort by brokerage firms to minimize the appearance of conflicts caused by commission-based selling.

A wrap account is a managed account, usually managed by selected outside fund managers. Investors are told this is a good deal because they are not being charged commissions and they get access to fund managers otherwise available only to very large investors.

They aren't told that these fund managers have no more ability to pick stocks or to time the markets than a "financial astrologer" or a hyperactive broker or advisor acting on his or her own.

In reality, wrap accounts are a way for brokers to generate significant fees for doing very little work. The brokerage firm typically pays 1 percent of the investor's assets to the manager(s), and gets to keep 1 or 1.5 percent of the investor's assets, split between the firm and the individual broker. The investor essentially pays 2 to 3 percent of his or her assets for the privilege of investing with a manager who has no better chance of beating market returns than mutual fund managers who charge a significantly lower fee—and you have seen how unlikely it is that even these managers can beat the markets.

It really doesn't matter if you invest in a mutual fund or a wrap account. If either or both are hyperactively managed, they are poor choices.

The bottom line is that the combination of higher costs, lower performance, and greater tax consequences make all investments touted as being able to beat the markets worse than a zero-sum game, which is why Smart Investors avoid them.

20

Brokers Understand Fees But Not Risk

Odds are, you don't know what the odds are.

—Gary Belsky and Thomas Gilovich, coauthors of
Why Smart People Make Big Money Mistakes

C ost is one of the two major differences between Smart Investors and Hyperactive Investors. The other major issue is the relationship between risk and portfolio return.

There is a way to mathematically measure how risky an investment or a portfolio really is. It is called **standard deviation**. It has been accepted as the most appropriate way to measure the risk in investment portfolios since the work of Harry Markowitz in the late 1950s. Markowitz won the Nobel Prize in Economics for his research—research those hyperactive brokers and advisors either ignore or don't know about.

I look at standard deviation in investing the way I look at the results of my blood tests. I don't really need to understand how the lab arrived at the numbers, but I do need to know what is within normal range.

In investing, the higher the standard deviation, the more risky the portfolio. Here are some general guidelines, using the fall 2005 standard deviation of the S&P 500 as a guide:

- Conservative investors should have a standard deviation no higher than 8 percent.
- Moderately aggressive investors should have a standard deviation no higher than 15 percent.
- Very aggressive investors should have a standard deviation no higher than 20 percent.
- No one should have a standard deviation higher than 30 percent, if that.

For most investors, that is all you need to know about standard deviation. And that is more than most hyperactive brokers and advisors know.

Go ahead, ask your broker what the standard deviation of your portfolio is. If he or she can compute it for you, right there in the office, without asking for help, I will be stunned. In any event, if the percentage exceeds these guidelines, Smart Investors should get concerned.

STANDARD DEVIATION measures the volatility of a security or of a portfolio of securities. Specifically, it measures the fluctuation of stock prices without regard to direction. Standard deviation is measured using a statistical calculation. It is important for every investor to know, and understand the significance of, the standard deviation of his or her investment portfolio.

21

Too Many Stocks,
Too Few Bonds

Investment policy [asset allocation] is the foundation upon which portfolios should be constructed and managed.

—Charles D. Ellis, author of *Investment Policy*

Another important factor in proper investing—after taking account of costs and understanding risk—is asset allocation. Asset allocation refers to the percentage of an investment portfolio held in each of the major asset classes—stocks, bonds and cash.

Many academic studies have shown that the vast majority of a portfolio's variability in returns is accounted for by asset allocation. Very little is accounted for by either market timing or by picking the "right" security within an asset class. Therefore, it is curious that all the hype you hear from hyperactive brokers and advisors relates to market timing and stock picking.

When is the last time your hyperactive broker called you for the sole purpose of discussing your asset allocation?

Most Hyperactive Investors have portfolios that are underweighted in bonds and overweighted in stocks. They are invested in this manner because their advisors have told them that stocks will outperform bonds in the long term. Younger investors are told that they should hold a higher percentage of stocks in their portfolios because they have more time to deal with the bad years and, over time, stocks will outperform bonds.

This is basically true. The annualized return of the S&P 500 since 1926 has been 10.4 percent. During this same time period, the annualized return of long-term government bonds has been 5.4 percent. These averages are before taking into account inflation and taxes.

However, there are long periods of time when this does not hold true.

Take a look at this chart:

HISTORICAL ANNUALIZED RETURNS
(Data Period: 1965–1984)

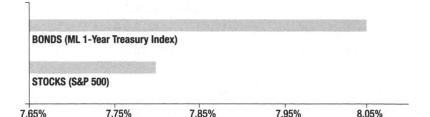

In addition, there is compelling evidence that investment risk does not always decline over time. Therefore, it is by no means always true that younger investors should hold most of their portfolio in stocks.

Bonds are an important part of your portfolio for reasons other than their performance relative to stocks. The performance of bonds does not correlate highly with the performance of stocks. This means that bond prices do not move in tandem with stock prices.

This is perfectly logical. The psychology of investing—often at the urging of hyperactive brokers and advisors—leads people to move money out of bonds when the stock market is rising and into bonds when the stock market is sinking. When the price of one asset gets low enough, there will be buyers who perceive it as "undervalued" and when the price gets high enough there will be sellers who perceive it as "overvalued."

When you have two asset classes in your portfolio that do not correlate highly with each other, you minimize your risk significantly.

The clear import of this data is that bonds should be part of almost every portfolio, in varying percentages. (You'll learn how to determine the correct percentage for your portfolio in chapter 37.)

Typically, hyperactive brokers and advisors ignore this truth. They do so because bonds are not as sexy as stocks. There is not as much opportunity for a steep rise in price. But it is because of this more steady, less volatile performance over time that bonds should be used as ballast in every portfolio, to keep it on an even keel.

Smart Investors understand that an appropriate allocation of bonds in their portfolios is critical to risk management.

22

Risk and Reward

The only way to "beat an index" is to invest in something other than
the index. Why would you, when the only source of long-term risk
and return data is the index?

—Mark Hebner, founder, Index Fund Advisors, Inc.

Everyone wants to make as big a return as he or she can. But at
what risk?

The possibility of gaining a few percentage points on the
upside may be dwarfed by the increase in downside risk.

Take a look at the chart on page 64, which illustrates this point.

As you can see from this chart, if you invested in a diversified
portfolio consisting of 100 percent stocks during the period 1973 to
2004, your average return would have been **11.19 percent**. Your worst
loss in any one calendar year would have been **20.15 percent**.

However, if you had a diversified portfolio invested in only 60
percent stocks and 40 percent bonds, your average return would have
been **10.49 percent**—only 0.7 percent less than the 100 percent stock
portfolio. However, your worst loss in any one year—instead of being
20.15 percent with the 100 percent stock portfolio—would only have
been **9.15 percent**.

By moving from a portfolio that is 100 percent invested in stocks
to one that is 60 percent invested in stocks and 40 percent invested in

RISK RETURN COMPARISON
(Data Period: 1973–2004)

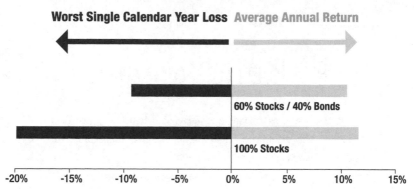

government bonds, it is possible to greatly reduce the downside risk while sacrificing only a modest amount of upside potential.

Is it worth it to you to squeeze an extra 0.7 percent on the upside, if that means accepting the possibility of losing an additional 11 percent on the downside?

Now, there is a classic objection put forward by those who are invested 100 percent in stocks or those who suggest that their clients invest 100 percent in stocks. That argument has to do with the long term versus the short term. It is true that, over the long term, stocks have a better return than bonds. Therefore, they argue, anyone investing for the long term should be better off investing completely in stocks.

There are, however, two problems with this argument.

The first has to do with timing. You never know when stocks will have a run of one, two, three, or even more consecutive down years. If those happen to be the years an investor needs to cash out of a major portion of his or her investments, or if the investor simply does not have the stomach to tolerate those losses, then the investor may be forced to sell at the worst possible time.

The second has to do with the basic fallacy of hyperactive investing. Hyperactive brokers and advisors often tell their clients to sell stocks or mutual funds that are on the way down and invest in stocks or funds that are on the way up. But in a market that is generally moving down, even the stocks or funds that are moving up may not move up enough to counter the losses in the previous investments, or may not move up for very long.

I will say that some Smart Investors—those who are investing in funds that match the broadest stock market indexes and who can commit *without reservation* to holding those funds for the long term—can safely hold a fairly large percentage of their portfolio in stocks. But I still don't believe anyone should be invested 100 percent in stocks.

Hyperactive brokers and advisors typically do not present data in this manner. Nor do they ask these kinds of questions. Their focus is exclusively on the upside. Timing the market, picking stocks and finding hot fund managers all speak to the upside. Marketing is all about the upside.

Smart Investors never lose sight of the downside risks.

23

Beware of B and C Shares!

There's almost no justification for selling B shares in large blocks.

—Douglas Schulz, coauthor of *Brokerage Fraud*

Most mutual funds sold by hyperactive brokers and advisors have different classes of shares: A, B or C shares. The reason for these different share classes is that mutual fund families have tried to figure out creative ways for investors to pay commissions that compensate these hyperactive brokers and advisors.

Class A shares have a front-end load, meaning the investor pays a percentage commission when he or she buys the shares. Most important, this front-end load percentage declines significantly (as does the broker's compensation) as the investor's level of investment in the fund shares increases. Class B shares levy a sales commission at the time of sale (a back-end load). This commission declines the longer the shares are held. Both B and C shares carry a larger annual marketing fee (part of the expense ratio).

For many investors, the reductions in A share front-end loads make that the preferred share class. However, hyperactive brokers and advisors have all kinds of convoluted reasons why investors should own B or C shares.

For instance, they tell investors that B and C shares have no commission. If pressed, they say that, yes, B shares have a "contingent de-ferred sales charge," but that this is less than the up-front load.

The real reason why brokers recommend B shares for large initial investments is that they get the highest initial commission for selling B shares. This commission is then offset by the brokerage firm keep-ing more of the annual marketing fee during the first few years in-stead of sharing it with the individual broker. After the deferred sales charge expires, B shares usually convert to A shares, with their lower annual marketing fee.

For most investors (except those who make a smaller investment—less than $50,000—and expect to hold the mutual fund shares for a short time—five years or less) B shares are a more costly investment option than either A or C shares. For small, short-term in-vestments, C shares are the best option.

For investors who intend to hold their shares for the long term (which is the way mutual fund shares should be held), owning C shares is the most costly option. For long-term investors who have more than $50,000 to invest, A shares are the least costly. While there is an up-front fee, over time the lower annual marketing fee more than offsets the up-front cost, and on investments of more than $50,000, the up-front load is reduced, generally going to zero on investments of over $1 million.

But some hyperactive brokers and advisors steer long-term in-vestors to C shares because the longer these shares are held, the greater their commission will be. This is known in the trade as "annuitizing" an account because the brokers and advisors use this technique to, in effect, create annuities for themselves. The large annual marketing fee keeps coming in every year—ka-ching, ka-ching, ka-ching.

All of this really begs the central question: Why are you buying *any* class of hyperactive mutual fund shares in the first place? And why would you rely on your hyperactive broker or advisor to select funds that will outperform the market?

Funds used by Smart Investors do not have A, B and C classes, so this is not an issue. That is another reason why you should be a Smart Investor.

However, if you insist on using a hyperactive broker or advisor, and that "investment professional" tells you to buy B or C shares, at least you now have the information to determine whether or not this is just another way to rip you off.

24

Beware of House Funds!

I find it very disturbing that Morgan Stanley's culture put sales contests ahead of customers. This is the kind of sales culture you'd expect at a used-car lot, not from your stockbroker, to whom you've entrusted your money.

—William Francis Galvin, Secretary of the Commonwealth of Massachusetts, August 11, 2003, commenting on a complaint filed against Morgan Stanley for sales practices concerning Morgan Stanley owned and affiliated mutual funds, for which brokers allegedly received higher commissions than on other funds

House funds" are hyperactively managed funds created, owned and managed by brokerage firms. They can only be sold by brokers who work for that firm. They usually bear the name of the brokerage firm that sponsors them (such as the "Smith Barney Aggressive Growth Fund").

There is no evidence that house funds are a good investment.

One study compared the performance of the house funds of American Express, Smith Barney, Prudential, Merrill Lynch and Morgan Stanley for a ten-year period with similar funds managed by well-known independent fund families.

The house funds got trounced.

Brokers typically earn a larger commission for selling these funds. It is not surprising that they recommend them to their clients.

There is no reason to buy a house fund.

This dismal performance record raises a much bigger issue: If the big brokerage firms cannot manage their own funds more successfully, why should you rely on them for advice?

The answer is that you shouldn't and, for that matter, you shouldn't buy any hyperactively managed fund.

Advisors to Smart Investors do not work for companies that own, manage or operate their own hyperactive funds. Because they don't work for companies with proprietary funds, they have no perverse incentives to recommend funds that, when objectively viewed, underperform.

Smart Investors never buy house funds, or any hyperactively managed funds. Neither should you.

25

Beware of Margin!

People want to maximize their return so they borrow to buy. And it can work, as long as the market doesn't go down. The smart money sells to the stupid money, and the stupid money usually borrows to buy.

—Charles Biderman, TrimTabs.com, a market-research company. Reported at
http://www.southcoasttoday.com/daily/04-00/04-16-00/d03bu127.htm

Warning: Margin May Be Disastrous to Your Financial Health.

When using "margin," an investor puts up the shares he or she owns as collateral against a cash loan that permits the purchase of additional securities.

Margin increases risk.

Since most hyperactive brokers and advisors don't know how to measure risk, investors who buy on margin are rarely aware of the effect margin has on risk. Margin magnifies risk—dramatically—by allowing an investor to purchase more of a security than he or she has cash to back up the purchase.

If the value of the security drops, the ratio of collateral to loan is reduced and the investor must either come up with more cash or sell some of the security in order to reduce the amount of the loan and bring the ratio back into balance.

Of course, margin is great for the brokerage firm, which charges interest on the margin loan. This may or may not be shared with the broker in the form of a bonus or some sort of "soft money" credit, such as an increase in the amount the broker can charge to the firm for individual marketing expenses. For the firm, there is no risk in margin. It is a pure profit center.

Smart Investors never buy on margin. They have no reason to do so.

26

Beware of Hedge Funds!

It's amateur hour in the hedge fund business. This sideshow of sometimes bizarre (and always costly) investing is on a tear like never before. It's attracting some of the shrewdest and sharpest minds on Wall Street—and also shills, shysters, charlatans and neophytes too crooked or too stupid to make any money for you.

—*Forbes*, "The Sleaziest Show on Earth," May 24, 2004

The "hot" investment of the twenty-first century is the hedge fund.

You need only be concerned about hedge funds if you have a large net worth, because they cannot be sold to investors who don't meet certain minimum-net-worth requirements. And many hedge funds voluntarily require a minimum investment of $1 million.

Hyperactive Investors have poured more than *$1 trillion* into approximately 8,000 hedge funds.

Much of the activity is generated by hyperactive brokers and advisors. They sometimes recommend investments in hedge funds to clients for whom such an investment is completely inappropriate.

This frenzy is driven by—you guessed it—fees.

Hedge funds typically charge 20 percent of profits plus 1 to 2 percent of assets managed. This is a previously unheard-of fee structure.

Brokers and advisors receive significant fees for recommending hedge funds to their clients.

The original hedge funds were pools involving few investors (usually fewer than fifty) who each put up a large minimum investment ($500,000 or even $1 million required). Hedge fund managers got the Securities and Exchange Commission to let them run these pools essentially unregulated by arguing that someone with that much money to invest is, by definition, a "sophisticated investor," and therefore hedge funds should be able to avoid all of the regulatory requirements that govern regular mutual funds and brokerage firms.

Many hedge funds specialize in making large investments in a few positions, which sets up the possibility for either outsized returns or outsized losses. Others have used a so-called market neutral strategy, which hedges these big bets with counterweight investments (hence the term, *hedge fund*).

All you need to know about why you should not invest in hedge funds is found in an article in the May 24, 2004, issue of *Forbes* magazine entitled "The Sleaziest Show On Earth."

For starters:

- The performance of these funds is often overstated. (In the summer of 2005 a hedge fund called Bayou imploded, costing its investors over $300 million. It turns out the fund never earned the gains it claimed it did, and covered up its losses by creating a fictitious accounting firm to audit its annual results.)
- Hedge funds are illiquid; you generally must leave your full investment in the fund for a predetermined period of time before it can be redeemed.
- You hear about the winners, but not about the losers.
- The cozy relationship between some funds and some major brokerage firms is troublesome.
- Hedge funds have an extremely short life span, averaging less

than 3.5 years, thereby depriving investors of the ability to analyze long-term returns; and

- There is no way investors can predict which of the 8,000 or so
  hedge funds might outperform a broad U.S. market index in the
  future.

Most investors should not invest in a hedge fund. For those who
do, the investment should be limited to a very small percentage of
their portfolio.

Hyperactive brokers and advisors love them. The commissions
are great.

27

Value Stocks—Reward Without Risk?

Most people want candy, when what they really need is a balanced meal.

—John J. Bowen, Jr., coauthor of *The Prudent Investor's Guide to Beating Wall Street at Its Own Game*

The term *value stocks* refers to stocks that trade at a low price relative to their "fundamentals." "Fundamentals" can mean factors like dividends, earnings or sales. Many advisors and authors of financial books—hyped by the financial media—believe that investing in these companies is a way to beat the markets.

Is this the magic bullet?

The short answer is a resounding "no!"

Supporters of buying value stocks cite data showing that value stocks, and particularly small value stocks, historically outperform other sectors.

For example, for the seventy-eight-year period from 1927 to 2004, an index of small value stocks had annual average returns of 14.6 percent per year. For the same time period, an index of large growth stocks had annual average returns of only 9.5 percent.

So, why not have a portfolio of all small value stocks?

Because of the risk—or uncertainty of returns—of such a portfolio.

Remember our discussion of the use of standard deviation to measure risk in chapter 20? We can measure risk with mathematical precision.

The standard deviation of a portfolio consisting only of an index of small value stocks during this time period would have been a whopping 34.9 percent. What does this mean in practical terms?

This means that this is an extremely volatile portfolio not suitable for *anyone*. The rare exception might be a very young person, with the ability to replace significant losses with ease. As you will recall, I told you that the most aggressive investor should not have a portfolio that exceeds a standard deviation of 20 percent and this portfolio (at more than 30 percent) is off the charts!

How volatile is this portfolio? Well, based on its standard deviation and historical returns, it is likely that, 68 percent of the time, the value of this portfolio can be expected to have returns ranging from an annual gain of 49.5 percent to an annual *loss* of as much as 20.3 percent. Is that enough to keep you awake at night?

Let's compare this kind of volatility with the high risk portfolio in the chart in chapter 4. This is the most aggressive of the four portfolios I recommend for Smart Investors.

Sixty-eight percent of the time, the value of this portfolio can be expected to have returns ranging from an annual gain of 24.9 percent to an annual loss of as much 3.0 percent.

Quite a difference from a portfolio consisting of all small value stocks.

The four portfolios I recommend give Smart Investors the benefit of the historical higher returns of value stocks, without the unacceptable volatility caused by over concentration of your portfolio in this sector.

Every stock in the market is either value, growth or some combination of value and growth. Growth stocks are typically thought of as stocks in companies that have rapidly growing sales, revenues and profits, and which plow most of those returns back into growing the company rather than paying a dividend to shareholders.

The market is defined as being equally divided between growth and value. Therefore, when you hold the stock market index funds I recommend in this book, you are holding half of your stock portfolio in growth and half in value.

No reputable advisor would recommend a portfolio of all small value stocks for anyone, except in the most unusual circumstances. It is just too volatile and risky.

And it gets worse. If you follow the advice of some financial gurus and use their special criteria for selecting a limited number of these stocks, instead of buying an index fund consisting of the thousands of stocks that are available in this sector, your standard deviation will increase, making your portfolio even more volatile.

Here is the bottom line: Investing all of your assets in any one sector of the market—especially a volatile sector—is foolhardy. It appeals to greed, but it is equivalent to rank speculation. The risk of significant losses is enormously increased. The risk of greatly enhanced volatility is all but assured.

Don't do it.

28

Why Hasn't Anyone Told You?

There are two kinds of investors, be they large or small: Those who don't know where the market is headed, and those who don't know that they don't know. Then again, there is a third type of investor—the investment professional, who indeed knows that he or she doesn't know, but whose livelihood depends upon appearing to know.

—William Bernstein, author of *The Intelligent Asset Allocator*

You have to give great credit to hyperactive brokers and advisors. They have told a story that feeds into human psychology at a host of different levels. They have successfully marketed skills they don't have. They are able to keep Hyperactive Investors so confused and disoriented that these poor folks don't realize there is a much better alternative. And by doing so, they have made a whole lot of money.

By all accounts, the average compensation of brokers is upwards of $150,000 per year, even in difficult years for the markets as a whole. This puts the average stockbroker in the top 5 percent of all American earners, making more than the average primary-care doctor, lawyer or full professor at an elite university. Not bad for someone who ignores basic principles of finance and is selling a hope and a dream, with precious little to back it up.

Conversely, advisors to Smart Investors have typically marketed well to large investors—endowments, pension plans and trusts—but poorly to the individual-investor market.

To be sure, there is enough money available from large investors for an entire cadre of these advisors to collectively earn a nice living. And it is much easier explaining the concept of Smart Investing to people who understand basic financial concepts, which many individual investors do not.

But those of us who advise our clients to become Smart Investors have been abdicating our responsibility to the millions of Hyperactive Investors. Perhaps it is because we have no financial incentive to provide this advice since, as I have said, most Smart Investors do not need our services to reach their financial goals.

The Vanguard Group, and especially the company's founder, John Bogle, are a notable exception to this rule. It was Bogle and Vanguard who created the opportunity for all investors to invest for market returns, by establishing index funds with low initial investments (as little as $2,500), low annual expenses and a coherent set of marketing materials.

While there are a number of books that have been written about the virtues of being a Smart Investor, few have achieved commercial success. There are a couple of exceptions. One is a superb book by Burton Malkiel, now in its eighth edition, entitled *A Random Walk Down Wall Street*.

Malkiel, a professor of economics at Princeton University, was one of the first to show that the history of the price of a stock cannot be used to predict how it will move in the future, and therefore that stock price movement is, in the language of economists, "random." In other words, he totally debunked the ability of anyone to consistently predict the future prices of stocks (which is the core belief of Hyperactive Investors!).

Most of the books and articles written on the subject are, unfortunately, dense and difficult to understand, thus, seemingly validating the myth that being a Smart Investor is somehow elitist, complex and beyond the ability of the ordinary investor.

Nothing could be further from the truth.

29

The Financial Media Is Part of the Problem

It is not easy to get rich in Las Vegas, at Churchill Downs or at the local Merrill Lynch office.
—Paul A. Samuelson, Massachusetts Institute of Technology,
Economist, Nobel Laureate in Economics

The financial media is part of the problem. In fact, the large brokerage firms are major advertisers in the financial media. As a result, the financial media are very dependent upon their goodwill. That means that the articles written in the financial media don't usually challenge the hyperactive broker or advisor's basic marketing thrust—trading.

Members of the brokerage community often are contributors to the "news" featured in the financial media. How many times have we all seen on television an interview with a brokerage firm analyst or "market strategist" where he or she is standing in front of the company's name? It's little more than free marketing. The guy could be reciting the New York City phone book, and it wouldn't matter to his firm. Every second that company logo is there in the background is thousands of dollars that doesn't have to be spent on advertising.

It is not surprising that this participation contributes to the popular image that hyperactive brokers and advisors actually add value and are worthy of deference from beleaguered investors. It is in the interest of the financial media to break news—daily, weekly or monthly—because they need to sell magazines or newspapers, or to achieve or maintain high viewer ratings. The financial media contributes to the false impression that investors must always be on top of the latest news, lest they miss an investment opportunity.

Some "investment" television shows are little more than tabloid journalism. Some self-styled investment gurus have resorted to behavior that can only be described as maniacal. This may be entertaining to some, but it should not be confused with any recognized principles of finance that might assist investors in making intelligent decisions about managing their assets.

Even the more serious shows encourage false beliefs—beliefs that are harmful to investors. The financial media, like astrologers, convey the message that predicting the future is the key to successful investing.

As ludicrous as this may be, it sells papers and it sells advertising time. In order to make sure it sells, the media publishes and airs no end of predictions from "experts" who appear, in fact, to know the future. We all have seen the stories, ranging from "The one stock everyone must own" to "The hottest mutual funds for next year."

But the advice they give is often erroneous and misleading. I give some examples of this erroneous advice in the next chapter, which is aptly entitled "Financial Pornography," because that is what it is.

Even if you find the financial media entertaining, you should ignore everything you read in the magazines and newspapers, everything you see and hear on the television and everything that you pay to have pumped into your Palm Pilot or BlackBerry that indicates that they can tell you where the markets are headed or whether or not a particular stock or fund should be bought or sold.

The financial media, with rare exceptions (like Jonathan Clements at the *Wall Street Journal* and Jane Bryant Quinn, the well-respected economic journalist) are part of the problem. Everything about them—from the ads to the opinions to the news—is nothing more than hype, masquerading as critical information that Hyperactive Investors must absorb in their quest to beat the markets.

If you become a Smart Investor, you don't need any of it.

30

"Financial Pornography"

> I was getting at the newspapers and magazines that make investing
> sound easy. "Three ways to double your money." "Ten hot stocks."
> The articles that make it sound like the journalist knows the right
> stocks or mutual funds to buy. And the fact is, we don't know. Jour-
> nalists don't have any business pretending they're investment ana-
> lysts. We can talk about stocks, investment ideas and what people
> are saying. But journalists shouldn't say that certain stocks will in-
> crease in value. Nobody knows. Soft-core though, the Net is hard-
> core.
>
> —Jane Bryant Quinn, August 1998 interview with ABC News

Financial pornography" refers to the endless predictions made in
the financial media. The term is generally credited to Jane Bryant
Quinn, who writes about economic issues in a syndicated column.

These predictions are intended to sell books, magazines and
newspapers, or to garner viewers and thus sell television advertising
time.

But financial pornography also serves to convince investors that
they can beat the markets if they buy the rights books, magazines and
newspapers, and watch the right shows.

The predictions of these publications and shows are often terribly
wrong and misguided, but they have served their intended purpose:

Hyperactive Investors continue to believe that the answer is out there somewhere. They just have to keep studying hard enough and pay attention to the financial media and to the hyperactive brokers and advisors who provide the predictions in the financial media.

In *Confessions of a Former Mutual Funds Reporter*, a former *Fortune* magazine journalist, who understandably wishes to remain anonymous, stated that "we were preaching buy-and-hold marriage while implicitly endorsing hot-fund promiscuity." Why did *Fortune* do this? Because "unfortunately, rational, pro-index-fund stories don't sell magazines, cause hits on websites or boost Nielsen ratings."

Here are some examples of financial pornography.

The July 1993 cover of *Forbes* featured an amusing picture of Barton Biggs, who was then the chief global strategist of Morgan Stanley. Biggs donned a bear costume for the occasion. The article featured Biggs's advice to sell U.S. stocks and buy the stocks of emerging country growth markets.

Following his advice would have been an unmitigated disaster. Emerging-market stocks plunged for the next three years.

In November 2000, the venerable *Fortune* magazine set forth the "top picks" from its panelists of "top" stock analysts.

Between November 2000 and November 2003, here is how those predictions fared:

S&P 500	−22%
NASDAQ	−41%
Fortune **Picks**	**−80%**

In August 1979, *BusinessWeek* featured a story entitled "The Death of Equities." The story, true to its name, opined that "the death of equities is a near-permanent condition."

Almost immediately after the story's publication, far from "dying," stocks began one of the great bull markets in history.

Books by other self-styled "experts" have fared no better. Investors who followed the advice in Howard Ruff's bestseller, *How to Prosper During the Coming Bad Years*, fared disastrously during the ensuing bull market.

And who can forget all of the bullish advice during the tech boom to focus on that sector and ignore investment fundamentals. Investors who followed the predictions and advice of these investment gurus lost up to 80 percent of their portfolios' value when the tech bubble exploded.

Sometimes they are right. Sometimes they are wrong. When they are right, it is luck and not skill.

Hyperactive Investors rely on the financial media both to suggest to them what they should do, then to validate what they have done. Why would you rely on a source of information that is so frequently wrong and misleading, and that has a vested economic interest in keeping its ratings up so that it can increase its advertising revenues?

More important, why would you go back to the hyperactive brokers and advisors who are featured in much of the financial media and rely on them for financial advice when the predictions they make so publicly are often without any basis in fact?

Smart Investors pay no attention to the predictions made in the financial media, and never use them as a basis for their investment decisions.

If you become a Smart Investor, you can still read the financial media—but only for its entertainment value.

31

Surprise—Your Broker Does Not Have to Act in Your Best Interest

Unfortunately, the SEC's latest decision leaves in place a flawed regulatory structure that lets broker-dealers tell clients that they are giving objective, independent financial advice when, in fact, they might not be doing that.

—Jamie Milne, chairman, National Association of Personal Financial Advisors.
Reported at http://www.emarotta.com/article.php?ID=130

As I mentioned in chapter 19, in recent years, brokerage firms have offered managed accounts. Investors in these accounts pay an annual fee for management services that are calculated as a percentage of assets under management rather than paying trade commissions.

Investment advisors also typically charge a fee calculated as a percentage of assets under management for managing investors' accounts.

However, the brokerage industry successfully lobbied for what has come to be called the "Merrill Lynch Rule," which provides a regulatory exemption for brokers to offer fee-based financial advice without being held to the same standard of conduct as investment advisors performing similar services.

This rule creates lots of opportunity for brokerage firms and their employees to exploit Hyperactive Investors. In April 2005, the SEC unanimously approved the rule clearing the way for broker-dealers to offer fee-based accounts without registering as investment advisors. They do, however, have to disclose to their clients their potential conflicts of interest by making statements such as:

- "Our interests may not be the same as yours"; or
- "We are paid both by you and, sometimes, by people who compensate us based on what you buy."

Why is this exemption important and why should the investing public be up in arms? Perhaps a better question is, why would you entrust your money to a brokerage firm that has these kinds of conflicts between its interests and yours?

Brokerage firms and their employees are regulated by not only the Securities and Exchange Commission (SEC), but also by the National Association of Securities Dealers (NASD). Under the regulations enacted by the NASD, they are held to what is known as the suitability rule—a product or service they offer must only meet the standard of being "suitable" for a client's situation—it does not have to be the product or service that is in the client's best interest.

For example, brokerage firm employees are not required to obtain "best execution" pricing for their clients' trades, which means they can steer NASDAQ stocks to market-maker firms that offer a "payment for order flow" kickback. They are also allowed to sell their clients a fund that is not the lowest cost, as long as it is a "similarly suitable" fund, even though it has a higher expense ratio and provides the broker with a larger commission or satisfies sales production requirements (read: house funds).

The new SEC rule regarding managed funds allows brokers to offer fee-based accounts to clients on a "nondiscretionary" basis, as long as any investment advice provided is "solely incidental" to their order-taking brokerage services.

Now, I don't know what you think when you read such non-sense. But to me there is no such thing as a nondiscretionary man-aged account. By turning over the account to an investment manager the client is, by definition, giving the manager discretion to trade in the account as he or she sees fit. It is clear to me that this investment advice is not "solely incidental" to order taking.

In stark contrast, investment advisors are governed by the Invest-ment Advisors Act of 1940, which places on them a *fiduciary* obliga-tion to act solely in a client's best interests, or face a lawsuit for breach of fiduciary duty. This is a much higher standard than one of mere "suitability." Indeed a "fiduciary" standard legally obligates an advi-sor to put aside personal interests, and he is required to act in good faith when making decisions for his or her clients.

Faced with the choice of working with a broker who is held to a mere suitability standard, or an investment advisor who is held to a fi-duciary standard, investors who require the services of an advisor (and most of you do not) should always choose to work with an advi-sor who is duty-bound to look out for the investor's best interests.

But most investors are not savvy enough to understand this regu-latory distinction. They can be lulled by their hyperactive broker into thinking that when they put their investment portfolio into a wrap ac-count they are moving from a brokerage model to an investment advi-sory model. But as long as the investment is made through a brokerage account, and not through an account with a registered in-vestment advisor, the investor is exposed to the possibility of conflicts of interest (which have to be disclosed) between the brokerage firm and him or herself.

I find it remarkable and, in fact, reprehensible, that hyperactive brokers used their considerable political clout to avoid being held to the highest possible ethical standard to their clients.

I realize this is hard to believe, so try this test. Ask your broker to send you a letter in which he states that he is acting as your fiduciary. Simple enough to do. I predict that he won't do it.

The infamous "Merrill Lynch Rule" is yet another reason why you should not reward this lobbying success by giving hyperactive brokers your business—or your trust.

32

Another Surprise—Your Broker Is Not Required to Be Careful with Your Money

This message (that attempting to beat the market is futile) can never be sold on Wall Street because it is in effect telling stock analysts to drop dead.

—Paul Samuelson, Ph.D., Nobel Laureate. Reported at
http://www.ifa.com/library/quotations.asp

Try this nugget out on the next broker or investment advisor who recommends the purchase of a "hot" stock or a "hot" mutual fund:

"The Prudent Investor Rule governs the conduct of trustees of pension plans, trusts and similar funds. Trillions of dollars of assets are managed by these trustees. So, do you follow the Prudent Investor Rule?"

After all, being "prudent" is a pretty low standard. It only requires your hyperactive broker to be "careful" when he or she invests your hard-earned money.

The Reporter's Notes to the Prudent Investor Act (often referred to as the "Prudent Man Rule" and adopted by all fifty states) sets forth the following:

> "... fiduciaries and other investors are confronted with potent evidence that the application of expertise, investigation and diligence in efforts to beat the market in these publicly traded securities ordinarily promises little or no payoff or even a negative payoff after taking account of research and transaction costs."

Translation: Investors should seek market returns and not engage in stock picking or market timing in an effort (usually fruitless) to "beat the markets."

Hyperactive brokers and advisors ignore this "potent evidence." Their daily grind consists of convincing you that they can "beat the market" because of their superior research and analytical abilities.

Check out the quote again. It says that this activity "ordinarily promises little or no payoff or even a negative payoff . . ."

If, when you opened an account with a hyperactive broker or advisor, that person candidly told you that he or she would be trying to beat the market but in all likelihood would not be able to and was actually likely to underperform the market, would you still do business with that person? Of course you would not. And you shouldn't.

Advisors to Smart Investors follow the letter and the spirit of the Prudent Investor Rule. They make no effort to time the market or to pick winners. They understand this "potent evidence."

You should follow their lead and do the same thing with your money.

33

The Perils of Mandatory Arbitration

The term "arbitration" as it is used in these proceedings is a misnomer. Most often, this process is not about two evenly matched parties to a dispute seeking the middle ground and a resolution to their conflict from knowledgeable, independent and unbiased factfinders. Rather, what we have in America today is an industry-sponsored damage containment and control program, masquerading as a juridical proceeding.

—William Galvin, Massachusetts Secretary of the Commonwealth,
Congressional testimony before the U.S. House Subcommittee
on Capital Markets, Insurance and Government-
Sponsored Enterprises, March 17, 2005

E very investor who opens a brokerage account with any brokerage firm in the United States has to sign an Account Opening Statement. These statements bind the investors to resolve all disputes with the broker in a mandatory arbitration system, which is administered by the securities industry itself—the NASD or the New York Stock Exchange (NYSE).

Welcome to the world of mandatory arbitration.

You don't get access to the courts.

You don't get a jury.

You don't get an unbiased tribunal.

In fact, one of the three "arbitrators" must be affiliated with the securities industry and the other two may have had past ties with the industry.

This means, as a practical matter, that one-third of the panel is probably biased against the investor at the outset and that this person will use his or her supposedly superior "expertise" to try to influence the other two members of the panel to vote against the investor.

As a result of this appalling deprivation of investors' rights, many investors who have been victimized by broker misconduct are victimized a second time when they attempt to recover their losses from one of these industry-administered arbitration panels.

Of course, you don't have this problem if you are a Smart Investor. Smart Investors don't use hyperactive brokers or advisors.

If you use registered investment advisors who advise clients to be Smart Investors, your agreement with that advisor might or might not have an arbitration clause. If it does, you should insist that the arbitration be administered by a totally impartial body, such as the American Arbitration Association, and that all of the arbitrators be totally neutral and impartial.

When you deal with registered investment advisors, you have the leverage to negotiate a fair dispute resolution clause. When you deal with almost any broker or brokerage firm, it is their way or the highway. You have no place to go and no leverage. Either you sign an agreement forcing you to submit to a mandatory arbitration system run by the industry you may be suing, or you cannot do business with any brokerage firm that is a member of the NASD or the NYSE.

This is a really disgraceful process.

Hyperactive brokers premise their advice on abilities they do not have. When, quite predictably, some of their clients are harmed by this advice and seek to recover their losses, these same brokers hide behind a process that many observers believe is rigged and biased against the clients.

Standing alone, the existence of this mandatory arbitration system is reason enough to avoid hyperactive brokers.

PART THREE

SMART INVESTORS
KNOW BETTER

34

Who Believes Me?

The $4.8 billion Orange County (California) Employees' Retirement System more than doubled its total indexed assets to $1.2 billion during the twelve months ended September 30, 2001, from $593 million the year before. "We think that (indexed) exposure was a reasonable portfolio for the return characteristics and compared favorably with active (management)."

—Farouki Majeed, chief investment officer, ASSETS UP 30%.

In Fred Williams, "Where the Action Is: Funds Embrace Enhanced Indexing," *Pensions and Investments*, Jan. 22, 2001

There is $550 billion invested by individuals in index stock mutual funds. But there is over $4 *trillion* invested in U.S. and international stock and bond indexes, when these mutual fund investments are combined with the investments of institutions such as pension funds, universities and foundations. What do the managers of these institutions' investment portfolios know that you don't? After all, they could hire any hyperactive broker or advisor in the world, but they elect not to do so.

Here is a very abbreviated list of institutional investors with large Smart Investment portfolios.

Pension Funds
(each one has invested over $50 billion for market returns)

- California Public Employees Retirement System
- New York State Common
- California State Teachers
- New York State Teachers
- Florida State Board
- City of San Diego
- City of Seattle
- State of Maryland
- State of Utah
- Los Angeles City Employees Retirement Association

Educational Institutions

- California Institute of Technology
- Carnegie Mellon University
- Cornell University
- University of Miami

Religious and Charitable Organizations

- Catholic Superannuation Fund
- Jewish Community Foundation
- Salvation Army

A number of professional money management companies that manage large pools on behalf of institutions as well as wealthy individuals also utilize Smart Investing. Among them are:

Fund Managers

- Barclays Global Investors—Managers of iShares, which are indexed to various benchmarks; Barclays manages over $700 billion in indexed assets

WHO BELIEVES ME?   101

- State Street Global Advisors—Manages over $400 billion in indexed assets
- Deutsche Asset Management—Manages over $145 billion in indexed assets
- TIAA-CREF—Manages over $100 billion in indexed assets

To me, what is more telling even than these statistics is the list of individuals who either are Smart Investors or who believe that individual investors should be Smart Investors. Many of them are quoted at the beginning of chapters in this book. Here are a few:

Nobel Laureates (Economics)
- Daniel Kahneman
- Merton Miller
- Myron S. Scholes, who designed one of the most sophisticated pricing models for valuing stock options
- Paul A. Samuelson, author of one of the most widely used texts in general economics
- Robert C. Merton
- William F. Sharpe

Professors of Finance or Economics
- Burton G. Malkiel, professor of economics, Princeton University, and author, *A Random Walk Down Wall Street*
- Eugene F. Fama, professor of finance, University of Chicago, and consultant to Dimensional Fund Advisors
- Roger G. Ibbotson, professor of finance, Yale University School of Management

Malkiel, Fama and Ibbotson have all done their work on the theoretical end of investing. But David F. Swensen, the Chief Investment

Officer of Yale University, who also teaches economics at Yale College and finance classes at Yale's School of Management, has lived investing from the trenches. He is the author of *Unconventional Success.*

Swensen has made his professional name by running Yale's endowment fund, which has had superior growth through years when the market was up and when the market was down. He has been involved in expanding the scope of the kind of investing done by university and other endowments, from venture capital investing to investing for social return within the local community, to even short-selling the market when he thought it was appropriate. Yet in his book Swensen says that for the vast majority of investors, Smart Investing is the way to go.

There are two other men famous for their investing prowess who counsel investors to invest for market returns.

Peter Lynch, the longtime manager of Fidelity's Magellan Fund in the 1980s and early 1990s, and probably the first of the "rock star" managers, is a fan of Smart Investing. This despite the fact that he is one of the icons of active managers, a person who brokers and advisors continue to use to discredit the argument that no active manager can beat the market consistently. Lynch did it year in and year out for about a decade and went out a winner, retiring from active management for Fidelity to pursue other opportunities. As indexes have become more fine-tuned over time, and as the flow of information about investments has become more widespread over time, Lynch feels that the opportunities to find market inefficiencies has been essentially wiped out. The market *is* the return.

Warren Buffett, the "Sage of Omaha" and still the chairman of the Berkshire Hathaway company, is another legendary stock picker. Buffett's investments in industries and individual companies have, for years, had the power to move markets. But again, Buffett believes that efficient information flow and more indexing opportunities lead to greater market efficiency. Essentially, he says, market indexing will, over time, drive more market indexing.

This theory was recently validated in a study that demonstrated that stock picking in the United States has declined from a high of 60 percent of the maximum fraction of volume in the 1960s to a low of 24 percent in the 2000s, and there is compelling evidence that it will continue to decline. The authors of the study were so impressed with these findings that they concluded that ". . . modern portfolio theory has won," meaning that markets are efficient and that stock picking is a fool's errand.

This is very significant, but it begs the essential question: If Smart Investing accounts for the majority of the volume of trading in the United States, why do most individual investors continue to engage in the discredited practice of stock picking? And why do hyperactive brokers and advisors continue to advise them to do so?

The answer is very clear: Hyperactive brokers and advisors have no financial incentive to advise their clients to become Smart Investors. Together with the financial media, they are complicit in keeping this data from the average, hard-working individual investor.

So, which investors have received the message and account for the majority of the trading volume that engages in Smart Investing? Smart money. Like pensions, trusts and corporate money.

If trillions of dollars—the majority of the volume of all trades in the United States—is invested for market returns, by the most sophisticated funds and asset managers in the world, shouldn't your hard-earned assets be invested in the same manner?

You can fool the fans, but you can't fool the players. Smart money represents the players.

The next time your hyperactive broker or advisor tells you about a "buying opportunity" in a stock or the next "hot mutual fund," ask him to give you a written summary of his background and training in finance or economics. Compare it to the credentials of the aforementioned Nobel Prize winners, scholars, institutions and managers of megabillion dollar university endowment funds.

Then reject his advice.

You want—and deserve to be—a player. All Smart Investors are.

35

When Do Smart Investors Need an Advisor?

The expected return of the speculator is zero.
—Louis Bachelier, author of *The Theory of Speculation* (doctoral dissertation)

Most investors have under $1 million of assets available for investment. So you can and probably should engage in Smart Investing using your home or office computer, or even just your telephone, ***without using any broker or investment advisor.***

Larger investors, with more than $1 million in invested assets, pension plans and trusts, can often afford to pay an investment advisor. And some investment advisors can add value by adding a layer of complexity and fine-tuning to the asset allocation strategies that I will talk about in the coming chapters.

This fine-tuning for market returns usually adds some measure of extra benefit, without taking on extra risk. But it comes at a price: the management fee charged by an investment advisor.

Some of these advisors add real value by putting together relatively complex portfolios that seek a premium over market returns by using a fund family called Dimensional Fund Advisors (DFA) (www.dfaus.com). (Full disclosure: I am a registered advisor and use

DFA funds for my clients.) DFA manages more than $100 billion for large institutional and individual investors. It does not engage in market timing or stock picking. All of its funds are passively managed, using a variant of index funds. DFA makes its funds available through selected fee-based investment advisors. You can find a list of these advisors on the DFA website.

If you decide to use an advisor, you should be wary of anyone who does not consider the lowest-cost options to implementing investment portfolios. The lowest-cost options typically include Exchange-Traded Funds (ETFs), Fidelity and Vanguard index funds, low-cost index funds offered by other firms or the entire lineup of passively managed DFA mutual funds.

DFA and its network of economic and finance consultants, many of whom are university professors and some of whom are Nobel laureates, offer passive portfolios that are slightly different than ETFs and the typical index funds offered by commercial mutual fund companies. These differences are due to the way in which stocks are assigned to indexes. True index funds are rigid. They require that the portfolio matches the components of the index exactly. The problem is that stocks that begin a year as part of a specific index may lose the characteristics that caused them to be assigned to the index.

For example, if a small-capitalization stock has a run-up in price, it is no longer a small stock—it is a medium-capitalization stock. However, it will remain in small-stock indexes until the next time the index is reconstituted, which usually happens once a year. The stock will remain in small-stock index funds that are rigid in their composition. DFA would drop this stock from its passively managed small-stock fund when it ceased to be a small stock, not waiting for the index reconstitution.

DFA also offers funds that concentrate on more precisely defined sectors of the market than other fund families. Think of it like ice cream.

Many investors divide the world of stocks into **GROWTH STOCKS** and **VALUE STOCKS**. While growth stocks are stocks of rapidly growing companies, value stocks are stocks in companies who's perceived value as assigned by the market is below the value assigned by the particular analyst. The notion of value is truly in the eye of the beholder. Some successful investors, such as Warren Buffett, have made a career of being "value investors;" finding "undervalued" investments and taking large stakes in them.

A **SMALL-CAP** stock is stock of a company with a total market capitalization (shares of stock outstanding times price per share) of less than $500 million.

With Vanguard, for instance, you can have vanilla (a fund that holds all the stocks in the S&P 500 index, which is often used in financial shorthand as a proxy for the large-cap sector of the U.S. stock market).

You can have chocolate (a fund that invests in the S&P index of U.S. mid-cap stocks).

You can have strawberry (a fund that invests in the S&P index of U.S. small-cap stocks).

Or you can have a couple of other flavors that invest in other indexes.

DFA, on the other hand, has index funds that invest in the stocks of all sorts of very exotic "flavors," or market segments. For instance, one limitation of Vanguard and Fidelity is that they don't offer index funds in the international small-cap and international value markets.

There is strong academic evidence that tilting a portfolio optimally toward **value** and **small-cap** equities will, over long holding periods, outperform the broader equity markets by as much as 1 to 2 percent per year. That can add up to a lot of money when it is compounded over many years.

However, I do not believe that this "bang for the buck," particularly when you consider the added costs of advisors' fees, is worth it for investors with less than $1 million to invest. For these investors, the portfolios I recommend in chapter 38 should more than satisfy their financial objectives. There are, however, well-respected finance professionals who would lower the threshold for using an advisor who can give investors access to DFA funds to as low as $250,000.

Hyperactive brokers and advisors argue that it is small investors who need the extra "handholding" they can provide because investing is so complex and the typical small investor cannot be expected to know how to conduct research into the best possible investments.

But in truth, small investors don't need advice on how to make complex investments. What small investors need is actually very simple to implement.

Everyone is always looking for something that correlates positively with superior portfolio performance. Every academic who has ever studied this problem has found two things that correlate with superior performance. One is low transaction costs. The other is appropriate asset allocation.

Investing with the goal of market returns and without incurring any advisory fees definitely meets the first test. I describe in the following chapters how investors can easily ensure that their portfolios are suitably allocated for their investment objectives and tolerance for risk. And for Smart Investors with less than $1 million to invest, this self-help strategy is the way to go.

PART FOUR

THE REAL WAY
SMART INVESTORS
BEAT 95 PERCENT
OF THE "PROS"

36

The Four-Step Process

**No matter what, buying stocks by buying the market through an
index is a good idea.**
—David M. Blitzer, chief investment strategist, Standard & Poor's,
author of *Outpacing the Pros*

Being a Smart Investor is very simple. Just follow these four basic
steps:

1. Decide on your asset allocation.
2. Open an account with any of the fund families noted in chapter
   38 (I have no association with any of them).
3. Invest the stock and bond portions of your portfolio in the
   funds described in this book (remember, even fund companies
   that have a good group of no-load index funds also have funds
   that are hyperactively managed, since most individuals are mis-
   informed and still want to be invested in these types of funds).
4. Rebalance your portfolio twice a year to keep your portfolio either aligned with your original asset allocation or to a new asset allocation that meets your changed investment objectives
   and/or risk tolerance.

That's it.
Read on for more details on each step.

37

Step 1: Determine Your Asset Allocation

Over 90 percent of investment returns are determined by how investors allocate their assets versus security selection, market timing and other factors.
—Brinson, Singer and Beebower, "Determinants of Portfolio Performance II: An Update," *Financial Analysts Journal*, May–June 1991

A sset allocation is the division of an investment portfolio among three types of investments—stocks, bonds and cash equivalents such as certificates of deposit. Asset allocation is the big decision you need to make. All the other decisions are small.

Stocks historically have provided the highest returns and the greatest risks.
Bonds provide significantly lower returns than stocks but at lower risk.
Cash, the term for short-term, highly liquid investments, barely keeps up with inflation, but is very close to risk-free.

By splitting your portfolio up among these asset classes, you can target the specific level of return you wish to get for the specific level of risk you are willing to take. Economists have very accurately modeled how different balances among these three asset classes affect both return and risk within a portfolio.

Academic research has shown that asset allocation accounts for 90 percent or more of the expected return from any particular portfolio. The specific securities held in the portfolio (stock picking) accounts for about 5 percent, and digressing from the ideal asset allocation to take into account outside influences on the markets (market timing) accounts for about 2 percent.

A number of factors go into determining your optimal asset allocation, including:

- Your age
- Your health
- Whether or not you need income from your portfolio
- Changing life events (e.g., divorce, death of a spouse, loss of a job)

Remember this general rule: the larger the percentage of stocks in your portfolio, the greater the risk. It is also important to appreciate the differences in the upside and downside potential of a very conservative and a very risky portfolio.

For example, for the thirty-five-year period ending in 2004, a very conservative portfolio consisting entirely of intermediate term government bonds would have had an annualized return of 8.5 percent and a worst twelve-month loss of –5.1 percent.

At the other end of the spectrum, an all-stock portfolio during the same time period would have had an annualized return of 11.37 percent and a worst twelve-month loss of –26.5 percent.

Ignoring your cash requirements (which financial planners suggest should amount to six months to one year of living expenses), almost all investors should have an asset allocation somewhere between these two extremes.

There are all kinds of formulas for figuring out your proper asset allocation. The most common "rule of thumb" is to take your age and subtract it from one hundred. The answer is the percent of your portfolio that should be in stocks, so as you get older you should have more of your portfolio in bonds (e.g., a thirty-year-old should be 70/30 stocks/bonds, while her sixty-year-old mother should be 40/60 stocks/bonds).

I find this formula too simplistic to be of any real use because it fails to take into account the many variables between investors of the same age (such as health and income) that could make the results of this formula very misleading. However, it is still better than the practice of many hyperactive brokers and advisors, which is to place 90 percent or more of their clients' assets in stocks.

There are also all kinds of questionnaires available on the Internet that you can fill out to determine your optimal asset allocation. Many of them suffer from oversimplification and are really not of much value.

I have prepared a questionnaire for those of you who want to validate your asset-allocation decision (see Appendix A). While it is not uncomplicated, you should be able to fill it out in about fifteen minutes.

A much easier and even quicker way to use this questionnaire is to go to www.smartestinvestmentbook.com, where it is programmed to be interactive, with all of the calculations performed automatically.

While no questionnaire, including the one included in this book, should be the only source you rely on to determine your asset allocation, my questionnaire is a reliable guide to helping you find the right asset allocation *for you*.

But in the interest of keeping things simple, let me say this: Most individuals would be well advised to use one of the following four portfolios (in ascending order of risk):

FOUR VANGUARD MODEL PORTFOLIOS
(Data Period: 1970–2004)

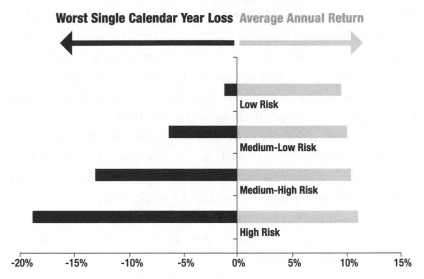

Worst Single Calendar Year Loss   Average Annual Return

- Low Risk
- Medium-Low Risk
- Medium-High Risk
- High Risk

In order to decide which of these portfolios is the right one for you, you need to understand the long-term history of the returns and the risks associated with each portfolio. In doing so, remember the future performance may not be the same as these historical numbers. But this is the most reliable data available to us.

Let's start with the riskiest of these four portfolios, which is the High Risk portfolio. That portfolio returned an average 10.96 percent during this time period. In its worst twelve-month period, it lost 18.70 percent.

If those kinds of losses in your portfolio would cause you undue concern, then this portfolio is too risky for you.

Now let's go down one level of risk and look at the Medium-High Risk portfolio. That portfolio returned an average of 10.50 percent during the same period. This return is .46 percent less than the High Risk portfolio. But in its worst twelve-month period, it lost only 12.65 percent (6.05 percent less than the High Risk portfolio).

I don't mean to downplay the significance of a .46 percent difference in returns. Over a twenty-year period, that could mean a difference of $63,400 on an initial investment of $100,000.

Now let's go down one more level of risk and look at the Medium-Low Risk portfolio. The annualized returns were 9.91 percent. Its worst single calendar year was a loss of 6.60 percent. This is certainly a far less risky portfolio than the Medium-High Risk portfolio.

Is this difference in returns worth the significant additional downside risk to you? If not, then you should seriously consider the Medium-Low Risk portfolio.

Now let's look at the most conservative of these four portfolios, the Low Risk portfolio. The annualized returns for this very stable portfolio were 9.22 percent. Its worst single calendar year was a loss of 1.69 percent.

Are you comfortable with historical annualized returns of 9.22 percent? If so, why would you want to assume more risk? If not, you should consider one of the other three higher-risk portfolios.

If hyperactive brokers and advisors presented data this way, most investors would have no problem figuring out what asset allocation was appropriate for them. But brokers and advisors rarely do.

Now you should have an asset allocation that is suitable for you. The most difficult part of this process—the most critical part—is done.

38

Step 2: Open an Account with One of These Fund Families

Most investors, both institutional and individual, will find the best way to own common stocks is through an index fund that charges minimal fees. Those following this path are sure to beat the net results (after fees and expenses) delivered by the great majority of investment professionals.

—Warren Buffett, Berkshire Hathaway chairman and legendary American investor, Berkshire Hathaway Inc., 1996 Shareholder Letter

Both Fidelity Investments and the Vanguard Group are well-known and highly reputable firms. At this time, they are engaged in a price war over who can charge the least for the funds that will give you market returns for each of the portfolios previously described. This is an excellent situation for you to take advantage of once you to decide to become a Smart Investor.

You can open an account with Vanguard by going to www.vanguard.com.

You can open an account with Fidelity by going to www.fidelity.com.

Each provider can handle taxable investment accounts or tax-

If you do not wish to invest using online services, both Fidelity Investments and the Vanguard Group maintain toll-free numbers, and Fidelity has some local offices. Consult your local telephone directory.

Fidelity Investments (for new customers): 800-343-3548

The Vanguard Group (investor and client information): 877-662-7447

T. Rowe Price (individual investors): 800-541-6066

favored retirement accounts (IRAs and Roth IRAs). There is a different set of forms for each type of account. For tax-deferred retirement accounts, be careful to use the correct set of forms; there are separate forms for new standard IRAs, new Roth IRAs and rollover IRAs. If you are rolling over a qualified corporate retirement plan such as a 401(k) or a 403(b) (for employees of not-for-profit entities) there is an extra set of forms you'll need to fill out for Vanguard or Fidelity to transfer your investments from the plan to a rollover IRA without incurring a tax on a retirement fund distribution.

In ten to fifteen minutes, you will be able to open an account. Both firms offer excellent customer support, in the event you need assistance.

Vanguard and Fidelity are not the only choices for implementing the Smart Investor plan.

Throughout this book, I have used Fidelity and Vanguard as the primary examples for two reasons. First, they are among the largest and most well-known fund families. Second, and more important, currently they have the lowest annual fees attached to the index funds that I recommend that you use.

A third fund family that offers the three types of index funds you need to appropriately invest your assets is T. Rowe Price (www .troweprice.com). T. Rowe Price is also a no-load fund family that, though not as large as Vanguard or Fidelity, does have a significant amount of assets under management.

If, for some reason, you do not want to use Vanguard, Fidelity or T. Rowe Price, you still have a number of other options, but it becomes a bit more complicated.

Unlike these three fund families, very few fund families have a single stock market index fund that spans the entire U.S. stock market. There are many fund families that have an equity index fund that matches the S&P 500 index. However, the S&P 500 index does not include small stocks. Since small stocks should be a part of an investor's exposure to the equity market, the S&P 500 fund by itself is inadequate. Therefore, you would need to find a fund family that has both an S&P 500 index fund and a small stock index fund.

The following are some of the fund families that have funds that would be suitable for this approach: Dreyfus (www.dreyfus.com), Charles Schwab & Co. (www.schwab.com) and Gartmore, which is part of Nationwide (www.gartmore.com).

In Chapter 39, I tell you how to implement the Smart Investor plan using any of the above-mentioned index fund options.

Finally, there is another option for you to consider, that does not involve purchasing index funds.

A fairly new, and increasingly popular, product is the exchange-traded fund (ETF). An ETF is a mutual fund that trades on an organized stock exchange, like the American Stock Exchange. ETFs are frequently designed to replicate the returns of a particular index, like the S&P 500 index and many others.

Because ETFs trade on an exchange, they can be traded at any time during the day that the exchange is open for business. In addition, the fees charged by ETFs are very low, which makes them a reasonable alternative to index funds.

However, there are some disadvantages to ETFs. Since ETFs trade like stocks, they also incur commissions like stocks. You will pay these commissions when you initially invest your portfolio, when you add to your investment portfolio, and when you rebalance your portfolio. When you use no-load mutual funds such as those I recommend from Vanguard, Fidelity or T. Rowe Price, you do not incur commissions.

In addition, since ETFs trade on an exchange, you will have to open a brokerage account in order to purchase them.

If you decide to use ETFs to become a Smart Investor, I will tell you how to do it in Chapter 39.

As a practical matter, it really does not make a difference whether you go the ETFs route or use index mutual funds. All that does matter is that you follow through and implement your Smart Investor plan, one way or the other.

39

Step 3: Select Your Investments

Surprisingly, one-third of all index funds carry either front-end or asset-based sales charges. Why an investor would opt to pay a commission on an index fund when a substantially identical fund is available without a commission remains a mystery.

—John C. Bogle, author of *Common Sense on Mutual Funds*

This is the easy part.

All we know about the stock and bond markets is that over time both will go up in value.

As I have explained, no one can predict which stock or which bond will increase in value, or when it will increase. And no one will know when or by how much the entire market will increase in value.

Therefore, investors should own the entire market. By "the entire market," I mean a broadly diversified portfolio of investments in domestic and international markets.

I have prepared the following charts for Vanguard, Fidelity and T. Rowe Price funds. They are very easy to follow and tell you precisely which funds to select, and what percentage of your portfolio should be invested in each fund, depending on the portfolio you have selected.

As you will note, I recommend that, for each of these portfolios, you take the total amount of the assets you will be investing in stock funds, and invest 70 percent of that amount in a domestic stock fund and 30 percent of that amount in an international stock fund. There is strong academic evidence that portfolios with some exposure to foreign markets have similar historical returns, *with less risk*, than portfolios invested only in the domestic stock market.

VANGUARD

COMPOSITION OF FOUR VANGUARD MODEL PORTFOLIOS

FUND NAME	LOW RISK	MEDIUM-LOW RISK	MEDIUM-HIGH RISK	HIGH RISK
Total Stock Market Index Fund *(VTSMX)*	14%	28%	42%	56%
Total International Stock Index Fund *(VGTSX)*	6%	12%	18%	24%
Total Bond Market Index Fund *(VBMFX)*	80%	60%	40%	20%
	100%	100%	100%	100%

If you decide to open an account with Vanguard, just do the following:

- Invest 70 percent of your stock allocation in the Vanguard Total Stock Market Index Fund Investor Shares (VTSMX).
- Invest the balance of 30 percent of your stock allocation in the Vanguard Total International Stock Index Fund (VGTSX).

The following is an example of the funds that would be purchased for an investor with $100,000, with a Medium-High Risk portfolio, who opened an account at Vanguard:

- ■ $42,000 would be invested in the Vanguard Total Stock Market Index Fund Investor Shares (VTSMX).
- ■ $18,000 would be invested in the Vanguard Total International Stock Index Fund (VGTSX).
- ■ $40,000 would be invested in the Vanguard Total Bond Market Index Fund Investor Shares (VBMFX).

- Invest 100 percent of your bond allocation in the Vanguard Total Bond Index Fund Investor Shares (VBMFX).

FIDELITY

COMPOSITION OF FOUR FIDELITY MODEL PORTFOLIOS

FUND NAME	LOW RISK	MEDIUM- LOW RISK	MEDIUM- HIGH RISK	HIGH RISK
Fidelity Spartan Total Market Index Fund *(FSTMX)*	14%	28%	42%	56%
Fidelity Spartan International Index Fund *(FSIIX)*	6%	12%	18%	24%
Fidelity U.S. Bond Index Fund *(FBIDX)*	80%	60%	40%	20%
	100%	100%	100%	100%

If you decide to open an account with Fidelity Investments, just do the following:

- Invest 70 percent of your stock allocation in the Fidelity Spartan Total Market Index Fund (FSTMX).

- Invest the balance (30 percent) of your stock allocation in the Fidelity Spartan International Index Fund (FSIIX).
- Invest 100 percent of your bond allocation in the Fidelity U.S. Bond Index Fund (FBIDX).

T. ROWE PRICE

COMPOSITION OF FOUR T. ROWE PRICE MODEL PORTFOLIOS

FUND NAME	LOW RISK	MEDIUM- LOW RISK	MEDIUM- HIGH RISK	HIGH RISK
T. Rowe Price Extended Equity Market Index *(PEXMX)*	14%	28%	42%	56%
T. Rowe Price International Equity Index *(PIEQX)*	6%	12%	18%	24%
T. Rowe Price US Bond Index *(PBDIX)*	80%	60%	40%	20%
	100%	100%	100%	100%

If you decide to open an account with T. Rowe Price, just do the following:

- Invest 70 percent of your stock allocation in the T. Rowe Price Extended Equity Market Index (PEXMX).
- Invest the balance (30 percent) of your stock allocation in the T. Rowe Price International Equity Index (PIEQX).
- Invest 100 percent of your bond allocation in the T. Rowe Price U.S. Bond Index Fund (PBDIX).

If you want more detailed information, I have included a more comprehensive chart (see Appendix B) that sets forth all of the relevant risk and return data for all four of the Fidelity, Vanguard and T. Rowe Price portfolios.

If you decide to use Dreyfus, Charles Schwab or Gartmore, you will need to purchase a total of four funds instead of just three. You should do the following:

- Find the fund that is the S&P 500 Index fund in the fund family that you choose, and invest 60 percent of your stock allocation in that fund.
- Find the fund that is the U.S. Small Stock Index Fund, and invest 10 percent of your total stock allocation in that fund.
- Find the fund that is the International Equity Index Fund and invest 30 percent of your total stock allocation in that fund.
- Find the fund that is the U.S. Bond Market Index Fund and invest 100 percent of your bond allocation in that fund.

If you wish to use ETFs, the easiest way to do so is to purchase "iShares." iShares are sponsored by Barclays (www.barclays.com) which was the first firm to offer a large array of ETFs. In order to purchase ETFs you will have to open a brokerage account. You should do the following:

- Invest 70 percent of your stock allocation in iShares Russell 3000 Index (IWV).
- Invest 30 percent of your stock allocation in iShares MSCI EAFE (EFA).
- Invest 100 percent of your bond allocation in iShares Lehman Aggregate (AGG).

NOTE: If you have less than a total of $25,000 to invest you may not be able to use these allocations because of minimum investment requirements for any of the above-mentioned funds. In these cases, you can adjust your allocations accordingly. Eventually, you may reach minimum investments that would allow you to make the optimum allocations for your profile.

40

Step 4: Rebalance Your Portfolio

Active management is little more than a gigantic con game.

—Ron Ross, Ph.D., author of *The Unbeatable Market*

Nothing is more important than your asset allocation. Therefore, it is important that your allocation remains where you want it to be.

But markets are inherently volatile, and the values of the individual investments constantly change. This means that every day your asset allocation drifts away from or closer to the original allocation you set.

Stocks and bonds may change value in opposition to one another. As bonds become more valuable, stocks may become less valuable, and vice versa. Over short periods of time, nobody can predict which way stocks and bonds will move or whether they will move together or in opposition. However, over the long run, stocks have returned more than bonds.

Over the course of six months, a lot can happen in the markets, and your investments in both stocks and bonds can drift quite a bit away from your initial asset allocation. An original 60/40 stock-to-bond allocation could be 45/55 stock-to-bond after six months if the value of stocks falls dramatically, or 75/25 if the value of stocks rises dramatically. Hence the need to rebalance.

Rebalancing can also be necessary because some life event has changed your need for income from your portfolio or your sense of how much risk you can assume in your portfolio.

There are two ways to rebalance your portfolio.

If you have an opportunity to add new money to your portfolio, you can buy more of the assets that you need to rebalance the portfolio. If you must work only with the assets you currently have, you need to sell some of the assets that are overrepresented in the portfolio and buy more of the assets that are underrepresented.

For instance, if your Medium-High-Risk portfolio now has 55 percent of its value in stocks and 45 percent in bonds, you are underrepresented in stocks and overrepresented in bonds.

Whatever the reason for your rebalancing, it should only take you forty-five minutes or so, twice a year, to complete the exercise, since you will only be dealing with three or four mutual funds or ETFs—U.S. stocks, international stocks, and U.S. bonds.

If you use an investment advisor, (s)he should call you up every six months or so to go over your portfolio, see if there is any reason to change your asset allocation, then perform the necessary transactions for you to rebalance the portfolio.

A number of firms, including Fidelity and Vanguard, have established model portfolios for retirement investments that automatically rebalance at regular intervals. Vanguard calls these funds the "Vanguard Target Retirement" funds. These funds have different asset allocations, depending on whether your "target" retirement date is 2015,

2025, 2035, or 2045. The funds are made up completely of Vanguard index funds, including those we suggest.

So if you don't want to carry out your own rebalancing, you can simply invest your retirement savings in one of the Vanguard target funds.

41

Don't Back Down

Wall Street's favorite scam is pretending that luck is skill.
—Ron Ross, Ph.D., author of *The Unbeatable Market*

Now that you have decided to reject Hyperactive Investing and become a Smart Investor, you need to be able to face your hyperactive broker or investment advisor. They are a hard-nosed bunch, with the thick skin necessary to be good salespeople. They have been rejected hundreds of times before, and have been trained to have a response to any objection a potential client could serve up.

So here are a few tips on how to face them down.

When you confront your hyperactive broker or advisor with the overwhelming evidence to support your desire to become a Smart Investor, you will hear some variation of one or more of the following responses:

- There is no "alpha" (meaning no value added) when you just invest for market returns.
- Smart Investing is for conservative investors only.
- We can pick stocks and time the market, or give your money to the top advisors who can.

Your response—assuming you feel the need to give one—should consist of some variation of one or more of the following:

- Being a Smart Investor will consistently give me the same returns as the market in general, less any applicable fees. There is overwhelming evidence that being a Hyperactive Investor will give me inconsistent returns. While some years I may "beat the market," other years I will not. Over the long term, my cumulative returns will be less than the market, especially when I consider the high fees, taxes and other costs involved.
- Being a Smart Investor is appropriate for both conservative and aggressive investors. What determines how conservative or aggressive I am is my asset allocation, not whether I am, or am not, trying to beat the markets. There are ways to invest in more aggressive markets (by increasing the percentage of stocks in my portfolio, for example) that can be extremely aggressive, but still produce the market returns for that market and, when owned in the correct proportion within my portfolio, do not add undue risk.
- You may be able to show me some short-term results, where a particular money manager has "beaten the market" three or five years running. But, over the long term, I will outperform the vast majority of mutual funds by being a Smart Investor, since academic research shows that that there is no way to predict which mutual funds will perform well, and which ones will not, in the future.

Instead of just being on the defensive, ask your hyperactive broker or advisor these questions:

1. What is my asset allocation?

If it is more that 80 percent stocks, and even if it is less than that, it may be too risky for you.

2. What is my standard deviation?

If it is more than 30 percent, and even if it is significantly less than that, it may be too risky for you.

3. Are you acting as a fiduciary in your dealings with me, requiring you to act solely in my best interest? If not, why won't you agree to do so?

If he will not agree to act solely in your best interest, you should not do business with him.

4. Do you engage in market timing and stock picking? What facts do you have that indicate that you or anyone else can do this successfully over the long term?

If he engages in market timing or stock picking, he is gambling with your money. What does he know that Smart Investors, who account for 76 percent of all trades in the U.S. markets, don't? Why are you part of the disadvantaged minority?

5. Why wouldn't I be better off investing in a suitably allocated portfolio of index funds or exchange-traded funds, with much lower expense ratios, than in actively managed mutual funds, over the long term?

If he says anything other than "You would," he either does not understand the data or he is not being candid with you.

Then walk out the door, close your account and become a Smart Investor.

42

Where Are the 401(k) Plans for Smart Investors?

... they [corporations] are simply unaware of the historical evidence, or perhaps they believe in the triumph of hope over experience and wisdom. In any case, it is the employees that lose. Employees should band together to demand that employers provide them with passive choices.

—Larry Swedroe, "There Is Trouble in 401(k) Land"
Index Funds Advisors article, July 16, 2002

For many investors, their 401(k) plan is their primary retirement vehicle. However, it can be very difficult to be a Smart Investor in many 401(k) plans, because many of these plans do not offer the appropriate choices of index or passively managed funds.

There are two basic reasons for this sad situation.

First, fund management firms frequently offer to absorb all of the administration costs of the plan if the company will agree to make the hyperactively managed (high expense ratio) funds of that fund family the exclusive or the predominant choices for employees. The ethics of this practice strikes me as indefensible, but it is very common.

Second, brokers and investment advisors are often advisors to 401(k) plans. Hyperactive funds sometimes offer higher commissions (or "loads") than these advisors could get from index or passive funds, thereby creating a classic conflict of interest.

Both of these factors work against the Smart Investor, who is deprived of the superior returns and lower costs offered by index and passively managed funds.

If you want to be a Smart Investor with your 401(k) plan, you should check to see if the Plan offers index or passively managed funds. If it does, you should follow the same basic strategies I have set forth for the balance of your assets, to the extent it is possible for you to do so.

More and more corporate, not-for-profit and state retirement-plan managers are providing Smart Investing options in their employee-directed retirement programs.

In a 401(k) or similar plan, Smart Investing options typically have the word "Index" in their name. Hyperactively managed funds never have "Index" in their name.

You can also read the description of the fund. For example, here is the description of the Vanguard 500 Index Fund:

"Vanguard 500 Index fund seeks to track the performance of a benchmark index that measures the investment return of large-capitalization stocks."

Contrast this description with the following, which describes the Vanguard Growth Equity Fund, a non-index fund:

"Vanguard Growth Equity Fund seeks long-term capital growth by investing in the stocks of mid-size and large companies with strong earnings prospects, and selling those whose earning prospects are deteriorating."

The Vanguard 500 Index fund merely seeks to "track" an index, typical of the description of index funds.

The Vanguard Growth Equity Fund attempts to pick stocks in companies with "strong earnings prospects." Read that as "stock picking." This is typical of hyperactively managed funds.

With these factors in mind, you should have no difficulty determining which funds in your 401(k) plan are index funds and which ones are hyperactively managed.

If you do this analysis and find that there are no (or few) index fund options, complain to your Human Resources Department. If enough employees complain, you will start to see 401(k) plans that encourage Smart Investing instead of compelling participants to be Hyperactive Investors.

It seems to me to be only a matter of time before a court declares that companies and advisors who have these conflicts of interest and resolve them against the best interests of the employees of a 401(k) plan are violating their fiduciary duty.

You can be assured that if there is accountability, there will be a change in these practices.

43

The Smartest Investor Who Ever Read an Investment Book

Some people change their minds because they want to, others because they have to.

—Howard Gardner, author of *Changing Minds*

Hyperactive brokers and advisors have a vested interest in convincing you that investing is terribly complex and certainly not something you can undertake on your own. Their agenda is to drive you to use them, so that they can convince you how they can "beat the markets" and, by the way, generate fees for themselves and their firms.

If you have read this far, you know that this is not true. These advisors are clinging to a discredited, minority practice, hoping that you will be too confused or distracted to find out that you are part of the disadvantaged, declining minority of investors buying into their "professional advice."

You can take control of your own investments with minimal time and effort—and by doing so you are likely to outperform the vast majority of these "investment professionals."

Specifically, this is what you now appreciate:

1. The single greatest threat to your financial well-being is the hyperactive broker or advisor;

2. The second greatest threat to your financial well-being is the false belief that you can trade on your own, online or otherwise, and attempt to beat the markets by engaging in stock picking or market timing;

3. The third greatest threat to your financial well-being is paying attention to much of the financial media, which is often engaged in nothing more than "financial pornography." This conduct generates ad revenues for them, and losses for investors who rely on the misinformation that is their daily grist;

4. Depending on the amount of risk you are willing to assume, as a Smart Investor, it is reasonable to expect your portfolio to achieve annualized returns ranging from 7 percent to 11 percent over the long term. Attempting to achieve returns higher than 11 percent involves speculating. If you decide to speculate, you understand that you are assuming a significantly increased risk of losing all, or a substantial portion, of your assets.

5. If you choose one of the four portfolios I have described, and invest in the funds or ETFs I have specified, you are likely to beat the returns of 95 percent of actively managed mutual funds over the long term.

Now relax and enjoy your life, secure in the knowledge that you have provided as best you can for yourself and your family.

You are now the smartest investor who has ever read an investment book!

44

Too Good to Be True?

So who still believes markets don't work? Apparently it is only the North Koreans, the Cubans and the active managers.

—From a transcript of Rex Sinquefield's opening statement
in debate with Donald Yacktman at the Schwab Institutional conference
in San Francisco, October 12, 1995. Available online at
http://library.dfaus.com/articles/active_vs_passive/

You know the old adage: If something sounds too good to be true, it probably is. It does not apply here.

People are always throwing around statistics and studies to support whatever they are selling. How do you know if what they are saying (or writing) really is true?

When it comes to providing support for avoiding hyperactive advisors and brokers and adopting the investment strategies I have set forth, there is an overwhelming amount of data. For those of you who want to do additional research to verify the statements made in this book, here is the underlying authority, but it by no means is intended to be an exhaustive listing of every study on this subject. I have organized it by chapter.

Since this is really a bibliography, which I know can be tedious and boring, those of you who are already convinced and need no further support can skip this chapter.

CHAPTER 1: AN UNBELIEVABLE CHIMP STORY

Information about the *Financial Times* contest was reported in the *Sunday Mail* (Queensland, Australia), March 17, 2002.

Commenting on her stunning victory over the highly credentialed "independent analyst," the five-year-old, Tia Roberts, thought it was "wicked."

She has a point there.

Studies that show the merit, or lack of merit, of analyst recommendations are nicely summarized in a paper entitled "An Empirical Model of Stock Analysts' Recommendations: Market Fundamentals, Conflicts of Interest, and Peer Effects," written by Patrick Bajari and John Krainer. You can find this paper online at http://www .econ.duke.edu/~bajari/analyst.pdf.

CHAPTER 2: AN UNBELIEVABLE TRUE STORY

I obtained the "100 million investors" number from the website for the North American Securities Administrators Association, available at   http://www.nasaa.org/About%5FNASAA/Role%5Fof%5FState %5FSecurities%5FRegulators/.

I rely on a speech by John Bogle entitled "As the Index Fund Moves from Heresy to Dogma . . . What More Do We Need to Know," April 13, 2004, for the statistics showing that over $7.5 trillion of the $8 trillion in equities held by individual investors is not indexed. It is also one of many articles that summarize the data indicating the historical underperformance of actively managed funds when compared to index funds, primarily due to the increased costs of the actively managed funds.

For details concerning the hundreds of millions of advertising dollars spent every year by brokerage firms, see http://www.onwall street.com/article.cfm?articleId=2401.

After all, it is not easy to convince you to buy an expertise they don't have!

CHAPTER 3: SMART INVESTING TAKES LESS TIME THAN BRUNCH

There is no better compendium of the "hundreds of studies" demonstrating the underperformance of active management than the one found at the web page of Index Funds Advisors. Go to www.ifa.com. Click on "Library" in the menu bar. Click on "Article Archives" in the sub-menu. There are 626 articles in this database. After reviewing the articles set forth there, click on "Books" in the sub-menu for a helpful listing of the books on this subject. Then click on "Articles" for a listing of the scholarly articles on this subject. Finally, click on "Videos" to see extremely informative videos discussing the perils of active management.

Great credit should be given to Mark Hebner, president of Index Funds Advisors, for this excellent website, which is an extremely valuable resource.

The June 26, 2002, issue of the *Christian Science Monitor* reported that stock market losses aggregated about $5.5 trillion in the prior 27 months ". . . or nearly three times what the U.S. government spends annually."

There are many studies that show that the vast majority of actively managed mutual funds fail to beat their benchmark over the long term. See "Will Active Mutual Funds Continue to Underperform the Market in the Future?" by John Bogle, from *Index Mutual Funds: Profiting from an Investment Revolution*; see also the article by Professor O'Neal, discussed in chapter 13, and a study by Dalbar reported at http://www .dalbarinc.com/content/showpage.asp?page=2001062100.

Burton Malkiel summarizes these studies in *A Random Walk Down Wall Street*, p. 187.

In Mark Hebner's book, *Index Funds: The 12-Step Program for Active Investors*, he sets forth the studies showing the lack of consistency of mutual fund performance and the daunting odds of picking an actively managed fund that will outperform its benchmark index, pp. 47–53.

One particularly compelling study referenced by Hebner indicated that, for the ten-year period ending October 2004, only 2.4 percent of the 1,446 funds that had as a goal beating the S&P 500 index succeeded in doing so.

CHAPTER 5: SMART INVESTING
SIMPLY MAKES SENSE

The study demonstrating the decline of stock picking in the United States is: Bhattacharya, Utpal and Galpin, Neal E., "Is Stock Picking Declining Around the World?" (November 2005), http://ssrn .com/abstract=849627.

A recent study with broad ramifications demonstrated that investors who selected their own mutual funds outperformed the funds sold by financial advisors, including brokers. Bergstresser, Daniel B., Chalmers, John M.R. and Tufano, Peter, "Assessing the Costs and Benefits of Brokers in the Mutual Fund Industry" (January 16, 2006), AFA 2006 Boston Meetings, forthcoming available at SSRN, http:// ssrn.com/abstract=616981.

The well-credentialed and highly respected authors of this study performed an analysis of the cost and performance of more than 4,000 mutual funds sold by financial advisors and selected by investors from 1996 to 2002. Here is what they found:

- Funds selected by financial advisors significantly *underperformed* those selected by investors on their own. The risk adjusted returns were *lower*;
- Funds selected by advisors were *higher cost* than those selected by investors on their own;
- Advisors did *not* provide superior asset allocation to their clients;
- Advisors did *not* prevent their clients from pursuing ill-advised investor behavior, like chasing performance.

You have to ask yourself, given these findings, why would you rely on these "investment professionals" for financial advice? It is bad enough that they did not *add* value. This study demonstrates that they *subtract* value.

CHAPTER 6: BROKERS MAKE MONEY WHEN THEY ARE HYPERACTIVE

The data for the performance of funds from 1945 to 1974 comes from the Bogle speech referred to in the notes to chapter 2.

There is an excellent discussion of the excessive costs of hyperactive funds and their adverse effect on returns in Mark Hebner's exhaustive book, *Index Funds: The 12-Step Program For Active Investors*, pp. 126–130.

Pay particular attention to the discussion of the effect of taxes that can cause investors to lose over 50 percent of their cumulative returns in the average hyperactively managed fund.

In contrast, investors in index funds lose only 13 percent of returns over the same (fifteen-year) period.

The bottom line is that index funds are far more tax efficient than hyperactive funds, which is another compelling reason to avoid hyperactive funds.

CHAPTER 7: A LOSER'S GAME

The study indicating that the average equity fund investor had an annualized return for the twenty-year period from 1985 to 2004 of 3.7 percent, when the S&P returned 13.2 percent, is a 2005 study prepared by Dalbar, Inc.

The data for the actual versus reported returns of the Fidelity Aggressive Growth Fund is derived from a study attributed to Charles Trzcinka, professor of finance at the University of Indiana, and reported in Mark Hebner's book, *Index Funds: The 12-Step Program for Active Investors*, p. 10.

CHAPTER 8: WHY INVESTORS PURSUE
HYPERACTIVE INVESTING

According to an article in *OWS Magazine*, December 2003, Wall Street firms spent *$428 million* in advertising in 2000. The misleading claims in this advertising onslaught are rarely challenged in either paid advertising or editorial comment. No wonder there are so many Hyperactive Investors and so few Smart Investors.

There are many studies in behavioral finance that support the statements in this chapter, which describes the reasons why investors continue to ignore the data and continue to be Hyperactive Investors.

An excellent summary of this research can be found at http://www.investorhome.com/psych.htm. There are useful hyperlinks there to the underlying research.

The entire history of the "hot hand" research is summarized at http://www.hs.ttu.edu/hdfs3390/hh_hist.htm.

The reprehensible conduct of hyperactive funds touting the "sizzle" of their past performance was recently exposed by the outstanding journalist Jonathan Clements of the *Wall Street Journal*, in an online column entitled "Those Performance-Touting Fund Ads Are Back—And That

Could Mean Trouble." You can find it at http://online.wsj.com/article _print/SB111395445960911421.html or at www.business.auburn.edu /~hinkech/clements.pdf. Clements is the rare exception to those financial journalists who routinely peddle "financial pornography."

Here is what Burton Malkiel has to say about charting (which he likens to "alchemy"), in his seminal book *A Random Walk Down Wall Street* (p. 165): "There has been a remarkable uniformity in the conclusions of studies done on all forms of technical analysis. Not one has consistently outperformed the placebo of a buy-and-hold strategy. Technical methods cannot be used to make useful investment strategies."

Malkiel believes that chartists simply provide cover for hyperactive brokers to encourage more trading—generating more fees—by their unsuspecting clients.

It is noteworthy that, in February 2005, Citigroup fired its entire technical analysis group. This was reported at http://www.shiau street.com/2005/february/18/ta.php.

If you are *really* interested in this subject, here are three articles that challenge the usefulness of technical analysis:

1. Fama and Blume. "Filter Rules and Stock Market Trading Profits." *Journal of Business*, Special Supplement, January 1966, 226–241.
2. Jensen and Benington. "Random Walks and Technical Theories: Some Additional Evidence." *Journal of Finance*, May 1970, 469–482.
3. Ball. "Filter Rules: Interpretation of Market Efficiency, Experimental Problem and Australian Experience." *Accounting Education*, November 1978, 1–7.

An interesting study of the relationship between speculative investors and gambling is: "An Analysis of Self-Identified Speculative Investors," by Richard Govoni, Robert E. Mann and Harold Wynne,

Journal of Gambling Issues, July 2004. It is available at http://www .camh.net/egambling/issue11/jgi_11_govoni_mann_wynne.html.

The study found that speculative investors who were gamblers fell into higher risk categories of gamblers than the gambling population at large. By extrapolating data from the group sampled, the study theorized that there would be approximately 456,000 people in Ontario, Canada, who are "self-identified speculative investors and gamblers." Of this group, 9,576 would be considered "severe problem gamblers" and 37,848 would be "moderate problem" gamblers.

These numbers are troublesome.

CHAPTER 9: THE "ACTIVITY" MYTH

The seminal study on the adverse effects of trading costs on profitability is entitled "Trading Is Hazardous to Your Wealth: The Common Stock Investment Performance of Individual Investors." It was published in *The Journal of Finance* (Vol. IV, No. 2. April 2000), and coauthored by Barber and Odean. This impressive study conclusively demonstrated a negative correlation between the amount of trading and profitability. This is not surprising.

By definition, hyperactive brokers and advisors encourage their clients to engage in more trading than investors need to do if they are simply seeking market returns. And "hyperactive" funds trade more than index funds. This increased amount of trading contributes significantly to the underperformance of these actively trading investors and funds.

CHAPTER 11: BROKERS AREN'T ON YOUR SIDE

The study of analyst ratings for firms that went bankrupt in 2002 was done by Weiss Ratings, Inc. It was reported in a speech given to the National Press Club on June 11, 2002, entitled "Crisis of Confidence on Wall Street." You can access this speech, which contains far more details about this study, at http://www.weissratings.com/crisis_of _confidence.asp.

Details of the $1.4 billion settlement with major brokerage firms involving allegations of analyst fraud may be found at http://www .sec.gov/news/press/2002-179.htm.

CHAPTER 14: NOBODY CAN TIME THE MARKET

The study on market timing newsletters was performed by two researchers at Duke University and the University of Utah (National Bureau of Economic Research Working Paper 4890, and published in another form in the *Journal of Financial Economics*, 42 (1996), 397–421).

Other studies have also debunked the myth of market timing. A very compelling one was authored by John D. Stowe, and is aptly entitled "A Market Timing Myth." *Journal of Investing*, Winter, 2000.

Alan Greenspan first used the term *irrational exuberance* in a speech entitled "The Challenge of Central Banking in a Democratic Society" on December 5, 1996, before the American Enterprise Institute for Public Policy Research in Washington, D.C.

CHAPTER 15: NOBODY CAN CONSISTENTLY BEAT THE MARKET

For an interesting study that discusses how trading costs can basically negate the value of analyst recommendations, see "Can Investors Profit from the Prophets? Security Analyst Recommendations, and Stock Returns," Barber, Lehavy, McNichols, Trueman, Graduate School of Business, Stanford University, available online at https://gsbapps .stanford.edu/researchpapers/Library/RP1541.pdf#search='analyst% 20recommendations%20underperform%20market.

The study quoted by Patrick Bajari and John Krainer is *An Empirical Model of Stock Analysts' Recommendations: Market Fundamentals, Conflicts of Interest, and Peer Effects*. This paper is available online at http://www.econ.duke.edu/~bajari/analyst.pdf.

CHAPTER 16: NOBODY CAN PICK "HOT" FUND MANAGERS

The short holding periods of investors in hyperactively traded mutual funds was noted in a study done by Dalbar Surveys, Inc., entitled "Quantitative Analysis of Investment Behavior," April 1994.

The same study noted that the holding period is even shorter (only two and one half years) for investors who "do it yourself," using online brokerage accounts.

This quest for the outperforming "hot funds" is obviously counterproductive. It only exacerbates the already-dismal odds against finding any hyperactively managed mutual fund that will outperform a comparable index fund.

The data on the lack of correlation between the Morningstar five-star ratings and future performance is set forth in a study coauthored by Christopher R. Blake and Matthew R. Morey, entitled "Morningstar Ratings and Mutual Fund Performance," December 22, 1999, available online at http://www.bnet.fordham.edu/public/finance/cblake/mstarv2a.pdf#search='Morey%20Blake%20Morningstar'.

Another study noted that funds selected by Morningstar for its own 401(k) plan significantly underperformed a broad U.S. market index for the period 1991 to 1999. The same study found that top performing mutual funds selected by *Forbes*, the *New York Times*, *Worth* magazine, *BusinessWeek* and fifty-nine investment newsletters studied over a ten-year period all underperformed the same index. Ravi Agrawal, "Active vs. Passive Investing," *A Research Review*, April 2004, available at http://www.rsaasset.com/whatwedo.asp?SPID=31427&OrgID=1040.

CHAPTER 18: HYPERACTIVE INVESTING IS EXPENSIVE

Information on the high cost of actively managed funds compared to index funds is set forth in the Bogle speech referenced in the notes to chapter 2.

The support for the discussion of the tax consequences of investing in hyperactive funds is set forth in the notes to chapter 6.

CHAPTER 20: BROKERS UNDERSTAND FEES BUT NOT RISK

Harry Markowitz was awarded the 1990 Nobel Prize in Economics. He is the author of the book *Portfolio Selection: Efficient Diversification of Investments*.

CHAPTER 21: TOO MANY STOCKS, TOO FEW BONDS

The seminal studies on the overwhelming importance of asset allocation in determining the variability of returns of a portfolio are: Gary P. Brinson, L. Randolph Hood, and Gilbert L. Beebower. 1986. *Determinants of Portfolio Performance. Financial Analysts Journal*, vol. 42, no. 4 (July/August): 39–44, and Gary P. Brinson, Brian D. Singer, and Gilbert L. Beebower. 1991. *Determinants of Portfolio Performance II: An Update. Financial Analysts Journal*, vol. 47, no. 3 (May/June): 40–48.

An excellent summary of some of the other studies on this subject can be found in an article entitled "Asset Allocation Revisited," co-authored by William E. O'Rielly and James L. Chandler, Jr., *Journal of Financial Planning*, January 2000.

For a discussion of why investment risk does not always decline over time and, therefore, it is not always true that younger investors should hold most of their portfolios in stocks, see an article entitled

"The Fallacy of Time Diversification," which is available in the Practice Notes section of the website of the Securities Litigation & Consulting Group, www.slcg.com.

This subject has been fully explored by a number of prominent economists who have persistently debunked this myth. For example, Paul A. Samuelson, "Risk and Uncertainty: A Fallacy of Large Numbers," *The Collected Scientific Papers of Paul A. Samuelson*, ed. Joseph E. Stiglitz (Cambridge: MIT Press, 1966), 153–8; and Zvi Bodie, "On the Risk of Stocks in the Long Run," *Financial Analysts Journal*, May–June 1995, 18–22.

CHAPTER 24: BEWARE OF HOUSE FUNDS!

The study comparing the poor performance of house funds to similar funds managed by independent fund families is based on data provided by Lipper, Inc., reported at http://moneycentral.msn.com/content/p27026.asp.

CHAPTER 26: BEWARE OF HEDGE FUNDS!

In July 2003, the SEC estimated that hedge fund investments would reach over $1 trillion by the end of 2004. As of July 21, 2003, the SEC had instituted forty-six cases involving hedge fund fraud, for a variety of unsavory practices. See SEC Release No. IA-2266; File No. S7-30-04, available online at http://www.sec.gov/rules/proposed/ia-2266.htm#P115_27303, July 21, 2003.

The sorry tale of the fraud involving the Bayou hedge fund is reported in an article in the *New York Times* on September 22, 2005, aptly entitled "Two Top Bayou Executives Plead Guilty to Fraud."

The risks of jumping on the hedge fund bandwagon were recently set forth in a sobering report entitled "Statement of the Financial Economists Roundtable on Hedge Funds," signed by a distinguished group of economists after a roundtable discussion held July 10 and 11, 2005, in Sonoma, California, under the auspices of the Stanford Graduate School of Business. In this statement, the economists noted, among many other risks and concerns, that the average life of a hedge fund is only "about three years."

The difficulty of evaluating the returns of hedge funds is discussed by Adel A. Al-Sharkas, in a paper entitled, "The Return in Hedge Fund Strategies," *International Journal of Business*, 10(3), 2005, available online at http://www.craig.csufresno.edu/IJB/Volumes/Volume%2010/V103-2.pdf.

Professor Al-Sharkas cites Lavinio, S., 2000. *The Hedge Fund Handbook*, as an authority for the short shelf life of hedge funds.

An article in the *Washington Times* on February 28, 2005, entitled: "The Bear's Lair: Instruments of Satan," stated, "It's very clear why ambitious hotshot traders and speculators want to run hedge funds; what is not so clear is why anyone would invest in them." This article is available online at http://www.washingtontimes.com/upi-break ing/20050225-020706-9695r.htm.

CHAPTER 28: WHY HASN'T ANYONE TOLD YOU?

For an informative discussion of the compensation of brokers, see "Reversal of Fortune: Compensation Trends, 2002" at http://registeredrep .com/career/finance_reversal_fortune_compensation/index.html.

CHAPTER 34: WHO BELIEVES ME?

You can find a list (current only through June 30, 2001) of pension plans that seek market returns through index funds at www.ifa.com.

Dimensional Fund Advisors lists the names of some of its clients at http://www.dfaus.com/service/clients/.

The information concerning the amount of assets represented by index investments from a speech by John Bogle entitled "As the Index Fund Moves from Heresy to Dogma . . . What More Do We Need To Know," April 13, 2004.

The study demonstrating the decline of stock picking in the United States is Utpal Bhattacharya and Neal E. Galpin, "Is Stock Picking Declining Around the World?" (November 2005), available online at http://ssrn.com/abstract=849627.

CHAPTER 42: WHERE ARE THE 401(K) PLANS FOR SMART INVESTORS?

In a report entitled "Staff Report Concerning Examinations of Select Pension Consultants" dated May 16, 2005, the SEC staff examined twenty-four pension consulting firms. Its findings were very disturbing:

- Half of the firms examined had clear conflicts of interest since they received compensation from both the pension funds they advised and the fund families they recommended.
- Thirteen of the twenty-four hosted "conferences" for the companies they advised, and most charged fees for the money managers to attend these "conferences."
- Ten of the twenty-four sold software to the fund families they recommended.

It is not surprising that, given these cozy arrangements, most pension consultants recommend high cost, hyperactively managed funds for inclusion in pension plans. The SEC examination is ongoing. This report is available online at http://www.sec.gov/news/studies/pensionexamstudy.pdf.

ADDITIONAL RESOURCES

A number of excellent books explore the subjects discussed in this book in far more detail than I have here. The problem I have with some of them is that they provide so much information, the overall message tends to get lost and cause investors to throw their hands up in collective despair. Unfortunately, the place they turn to for assistance is—you guessed it—the local hyperactive broker or advisor, who is only too pleased to "assist."

Nevertheless, for those who want to delve deeper, here are some of the best resources:

A Random Walk Down Wall Street, Burton Malkiel. New York: W.W. Norton & Company, 8th edition, 2006.

Index Funds: The 12-Step Program for Active Investors, Mark T. Hebner. Newport Beach, CA: IFA Publishing, 2005.

Bogle on Mutual Funds, John Bogle. New York: McGraw-Hill, 1993.

The Four Pillars of Investing, William Bernstein. New York: McGraw-Hill, 2002.

The Only Guide to a Winning Investment Strategy You'll Ever Need, Larry Swedroe. New York: St. Martin's Press, 2005.

Unconventional Success: A Fundamental Approach to Personal Investment, David F. Swensen. New York: Free Press, 2005.

And for those who believe they have been the victim of misconduct by brokers, advisors, and others who work within the system, and want redress for their losses, my previous book is helpful.

Does Your Broker Owe You Money?, Daniel R. Solin. New York: Perigee, 2006.

The website for this book, www.smartestinvestmentbook.com, is also a good source of additional information and helpful resources.

The website of Index Funds Advisors, www.ifa.com, is the preeminent source on the internet for the most exhaustive information and research on the subject matter of this book. I highly recommend it.

ACKNOWLEDGMENTS

It takes a village to write a book and this book is no exception.

I benefitted greatly from the insights of John Duff, my publisher at Perigee Books.

This is the second book I have written with the invaluable assistance of Jon Zonderman.

Carol Mann, of the Carol Mann Agency, believed in this book and was a wonderful source of encouragement and support.

Edward S. O'Neal, Ph.D., helped me understand and explain the more technical aspects of finance.

Mark T. Hebner graciously gave me permission to use many of the quotes, which are among those that can be found at Mark's stellar website, www.ifa.com.

Andrew M. Solin of Financial Graphics is responsible for the clarity of the charts in this book.

Sabrina Weill, a talented author herself, was a source of meaningful guidance and advice.

Mandy Solin spent countless hours assisting with design issues and providing much needed perspective.

My cover designer, Jason Arbuckle, patiently tolerated numerous suggestions and revisions.

My proofreader and Word expert, Nidhi Jain, expertly reformatted many drafts of the manuscript.

My wife, Patricia Solin, read and reread the text, and made a significant contribution to the final product.

APPENDIX A

Asset Allocation Questionnaire

This questionnaire will help guide you to a proper asset allocation for your retirement portfolio. This is only meant to be a guide. For each individual investor, there are many factors that cannot possibly be addressed in a generic questionnaire.

STEP 1: Add up all of the money that you currently have saved for retirement. This should include 401(k) plans, 403(b) plans, IRAs or any other accounts you are using to save for retirement. Write this number down here:

Current Retirement Savings _____   _____ **A**

STEP 2: What are your annual living expenses?

Annual Living Expenses _____   _____ **B**

STEP 3: At what annual rate do you expect your salary to grow for the foreseeable future?

Annual Salary Growth Rate _____   _____ **C**

STEP 4: How much are you contributing (in dollars) to retirement plans or any other accounts you are planning to use for retirement? Include your contributions to all retirement plans and also include any matching contributions from your employer.

Annual Retirement Contributions _____   _____ **D**

STEP 5: RATIO OF CURRENT RETIREMENT SAVINGS TO ANNUAL LIVING EXPENSES

Divide the figure in Step 1 by the figure in Step 2. For example, if you have $250,000 currently saved for retirement and your living expenses are $50,000, this ratio would be 5.

$$\frac{\text{Current Retirement Savings (A)}}{\text{Annual Living Expenses (B)}} = \underline{\hspace{3cm}}$$

STEP 6: Figure out how many years you have until retirement. For example, if you are 55 and plan to retire at 70, you have 15 years until retirement.

Years Until Retirement   = \underline{\hspace{3cm}}

STEP 7: SAVINGS-AGE SCORE (SAS)

On the matrix below, find the intersection of your years to retirement (found in the far left column) and your ratio of current retirement savings to annual living expenses (found across the top). Identify the number in this cell. This is your "Savings-Age Score" (SAS). To continue the example, if your ratio of current retirement savings to annual living expenses was 5 and you plan to retire in 15 years, your SAS would be 30.

SAS SCORE = \underline{\hspace{2cm}}

How many years before Retirement?	Ratio of current retirement savings to annual living expenses											
	<1	1–2	2–4	4–6	6–8	8–10	10–12	12–14	14–16	16–18	18–20	>20
41 to 45 years	80	78	72	60	40	28	20	12	8	4	2	0
36 to 40 years	76	74	68	57	38	27	19	11	8	4	2	0
31 to 35 years	72	71	65	54	36	25	18	11	7	4	1	0
26 to 30 years	68	67	61	51	34	24	17	10	7	3	1	0
21 to 25 years	56	55	50	42	28	20	14	8	6	3	1	0
16 to 20 years	48	47	43	36	24	17	12	7	5	2	1	0
11 to 15 years	40	39	36	30	20	14	10	6	4	2	1	0
6 to 10 years	24	24	22	18	12	8	6	4	2	1	0	0
1 to 5 years	16	16	14	12	8	6	4	2	2	1	0	0
Retired	8	8	7	6	4	3	2	1	1	0	0	0

STEP 8: Ratio of Annual Retirement Contributions to Annual Living Expenses

Divide the figure in Step 4 by the figure in Step 2. For example, if you contribute $5,000 per year to IRAs and your 401(k) (the $5,000 includes your employer's matching contributions) and your annual living expenses were $50,000, this number would be 10%.

$$\frac{\text{Annual Retirement Contributions (D)}}{\text{Annual Living Expenses (B)}} = \underline{\hspace{2cm}}$$

STEP 9: GCS

On the matrix below, find the intersection of your annual salary growth rate (found in the far left column) and your ratio of annual retirement contributions to annual living expenses (found across the top). Identify the number in this cell. This is your "Growth-Contribution Score (GCS)."

GCS SCORE = _____

Annual Growth of Current Salary	Ratio of annual retirement contributions to annual living expenses								
	0%	1–3%	3–5%	5–8%	8–10%	10–15%	15–20%	20–25%	>25%
8%+	15	15	14	11	8	5	4	2	2
5%-8%	14	14	13	11	7	5	4	2	1
3%-5%	14	13	12	10	7	5	3	2	1
1%-3%	13	12	11	10	6	4	3	2	1
0%-1%	11	10	9	8	5	4	3	2	1
0%	9	9	8	7	5	3	2	1	1

STEP 10: Risk Assessment Score (RAS)

Answer the following ten questions. Next to each answer for every question, there is a number. When you decide which answer is right for you, make note of the number next to the answer. Once you have finished all of the questions, add up these numbers. All of these numbers added together will give you your Risk Assessment Score (RAS).

1. **In addition to your long-term investments, approximately how many months of your current expenses do you have set aside in cash or money market funds for unexpected needs?**

A. 6 months 3
B. 4 months 2
C. 2 months 1
D. None 0

2. **How many years have you been investing in the stock market?**
   A. None 0
   B. Less than 1 year 1
   C. More than 1 but less than 5 years 2
   D. More than 5 but less than 10 years 3
   E. 10 years or more 4

3. **I consider myself to be knowledgeable about investments and financial matters.**
   A. Strongly Agree 4
   B. Agree 3
   C. Somewhat Agree 2
   D. Disagree 1
   E. Strongly Disagree 0

How do you feel about the following statements?
4. **I want my investments to be risk-free.**
   Note: Investments with no risk have little or no expected return
   beyond the rate of inflation.
   A. Strongly Agree 0
   B. Agree 0
   C. Somewhat Agree 1
   D. Disagree 3
   E. Strongly Disagree 4

5. **I am willing to expose my investment portfolio to some degree of risk in order to increase the likelihood of higher returns.**
   A. Strongly Agree 4
   B. Agree 3
   C. Somewhat Agree 2
   D. Disagree 0
   E. Strongly Disagree 0

6. **I am comfortable with a portion of my portfolio being invested internationally.**
   A. Strongly Agree 4
   B. Agree 3
   C. Somewhat Agree 2
   D. Disagree 1
   E. Strongly Disagree 0

7. **When my investment portfolio declines, I begin to think about selling off some of my positions and reinvesting at some later date.**
   A. Strongly Agree 0
   B. Agree 1
   C. Somewhat Agree 2
   D. Disagree 3
   E. Strongly Disagree 4

8. **Some investors hold portfolios that consist entirely of stocks. Such investors lost approximately 20 percent of their portfolios in October 1987. If you owned a risky investment that fell by 20 percent over a very short period, what would you do?**
   A. Sell all the remaining investment 0
   B. Sell 75% of the remaining investment 0
   C. Sell 50% of the remaining investment 1
   D. Sell 25% of the remaining investment 2
   E. Hold on to the investment 4

9. **What is the worst twelve-month percentage loss you would tolerate for your long-term investments, beyond which you would sell some or all of your investment?**
   A. 24% 4
   B. 16% 3
   C. 12% 2
   D. 8% 1
   E. Zero; any loss is unacceptable to me 0

10. **Based on $100,000 invested since 1975, the following choices show the highest twelve-month gain and the highest twelve-month loss of five different index portfolios. Which portfolio would you choose?**

    Note: The portfolios with the widest range between the loss and the gain also have higher average returns.

    A. Loss of $560; Gain of $23,500. 0
    B. Loss of $5,100; Gain of $31,000 1
    C. Loss of $10,500; Gain of $42,700 2
    D. Loss of $15,700; Gain of $51,600 3
    E. Loss of $22,200; Gain of $63,100 4

RAS SCORE = _____

STEP 11: PORTFOLIO ALLOCATION SCORE (PAS) [SAS + GCS + RAS]

Add your Savings-Age Score (SAS), your Growth-Contribution Score (GCS) and your Risk Assessment Score (RAS). This number is your Portfolio Allocation Score (PAS). Find where your score lies in the distribution below. The matrix below gives you a range for the stock portion of your allocation. Your recommended percentage allocated to stocks in most cases would be in this range. Once you choose the percentage allocation to stocks, the remainder will be invested in bonds. Of the amount allocated to stocks, remember that 70 percent of that amount should be in U.S. stocks and 30 percent of that amount should be in international stocks.

PAS SCORE = _____

% Stocks		
PAS	**Upper Boundary**	**Lower Boundary**
80–120	90	70
70–79	80	60
60–69	70	50
50–59	60	40
40–49	50	30
30–39	40	20
20–29	30	10
10–19	20	0
0–9	10	0

APPENDIX B

Risk and Return Summary

RISK AND RETURN SUMMARY OF
FOUR VANGUARD MODEL PORTFOLIOS

	LOW RISK 20/80	MEDIUM-LOW RISK 40/60	MEDIUM-HIGH RISK 60/40	HIGH RISK 80/20
Average Annual Return (Geometric)	9.06%	9.77%	10.38%	10.86%
Annualized Standard Deviation	6.86%	8.40%	10.87%	13.77%
Worst Single-Calendar Year	−1.69%	−6.60%	−12.65%	−18.70%
Worst Two-Calendar-Year Period	−0.32%	−10.28%	−19.74%	−28.69%
Worst Three-Calendar-Year Period	8.17%	−1.21%	−15.03%	−27.51%

COMPOSITION OF FOUR VANGUARD MODEL PORTFOLIOS

FUND NAME	LOW RISK 20/80	MEDIUM-LOW RISK 40/60	MEDIUM-HIGH RISK 60/40	HIGH RISK 80/20
Total Stock Market Index Fund (VTSMX)	14%	28%	42%	56%
Total International Stock Index Fund (VGTSX)	6%	12%	18%	24%
Total Bond Index Fund (VBMFX)	80%	60%	40%	20%

Raw Data used to produce performance numbers:
Vanguard Total Stock Index
    1993–2005: actual fund returns
    1976–1992: Wilshire 5000 Index −.25% per year
    1970–1975: (.85*S&P 500 + .15*CRSP Sm. Co Index) −.25% per year
Vanguard Total International Stock Index
    1997–2005: actual fund returns
    1970–1996: MSCI EAFE Index −.35% per year
Vanguard Total Bond Market Index
    1987–2005: actual fund returns
    1976–1986: Lehman Bros. Aggregate Bond Index −.32% per year
    1970–1975: CRSP Intermediate Term Gov't Bond Index −.32% per year

RISK AND RETURN SUMMARY OF
FOUR FIDELITY MODEL PORTFOLIOS

	LOW RISK 20/80	MEDIUM-LOW RISK 40/60	MEDIUM-HIGH RISK 60/40	HIGH RISK 80/20
Average Annual Return (Geometric)	9.16%	9.85%	10.42%	10.88%
Annualized Standard Deviation	6.87%	8.42%	10.89%	13.81%
Worst Single-Calendar Year	−1.67%	−6.69%	−12.71%	−18.74%
Worst Two-Calendar-Year Period	−0.53%	−10.44%	−19.86%	−28.77%
Worst Three-Calendar-Year Period	7.85%	−.50%	−14.82%	−27.71%

COMPOSITION OF FOUR FIDELITY MODEL PORTFOLIOS

FUND NAME	LOW RISK 20/80	MEDIUM- LOW RISK 40/60	MEDIUM- HIGH RISK 60/40	HIGH RISK 80/20
Fidelity Spartan Total Market Index Fund *(FSTMX)*	14%	28%	42%	56%
Fidelity Spartan International Index Fund *(FSIIX)*	6%	12%	18%	24%
Fidelity U.S. Bond Index Fund *(FBIDX)*	80%	60%	40%	20%

Raw Data used to produce performance numbers:
Fidelity Spartan Total Market Index
     1998–2005: actual fund returns
     1976–1997: Wilshire 5000 Index –.25% per year
     1970–1975: (.85*S&P 500 + .15*CRSP Sm. Co Index) –.25% per year
Fidelity Spartan International Index
     1998–2005: actual fund returns
     1970–1997: MSCI EAFE Index –.35% per year
Fidelity U.S. Bond Index
     1991–2005: actual fund returns
     1976–1990: Lehman Bros. Aggregate Bond Index –.32% per year
     1970–1975: CRSP Intermediate Term Gov't Bond Index –.32% per year

RISK AND RETURN SUMMARY OF FOUR
T. ROWE PRICE MODEL PORTFOLIOS

	LOW RISK 20/80	MEDIUM-LOW RISK 40/60	MEDIUM-HIGH RISK 60/40	HIGH RISK 80/20
Average Annual Return (Geometric)	8.99%	9.68%	10.26%	10.72%
Annualized Standard Deviation	6.91%	8.44%	10.88%	13.76%
Worst Single-Calendar Year	−2.19%	−6.73%	−12.80%	−18.86%
Worst Two-Calendar-Year Period	−0.55%	−10.53%	−20.00%	−28.97%
Worst Three-Calendar-Year Period	7.81%	−1.28%	−15.15%	−27.66%

COMPOSITION OF FOUR T. ROWE PRICE MODEL PORTFOLIOS

FUND NAME	LOW RISK 20/80	MEDIUM-LOW RISK 40/60	MEDIUM-HIGH RISK 60/40	HIGH RISK 80/20
T. Rowe Price Total Equity Market Index	14%	28%	42%	56%
T. Rowe Price International Equity Index	6%	12%	18%	24%
T. Rowe Price U.S. Bond Index	80%	60%	40%	20%

Raw Data used to produce performance numbers:
T. Rowe Price International Equity Index
        2001–2005: actual fund returns
        1970–2000: MSCI EAFE Index −.50% per year
T. Rowe Price Total Equity Market Index
        1999–2005: actual fund returns
        1976–1998: Wilshire 5000 Index −.40% per year
        1970–75: (.85*S&P 500 + .15*CRSP Sm. Co Index) −.40% per year

T. Rowe Price U.S. Bond Index

    2001–2005: actual fund returns

    1976–2000: Lehman Bros. Aggregate Bond Index –.30% per year

    1970–75: CRSP Intermediate Term Gov't Bond Index –.30% per year

PUBLISHER'S NOTE

accuracy, reliability, or thoroughness of any referenced information, product, or service. Any opinions, advice, statements, services, offers, or other information or content expressed or made available by third parties are those of the author(s) or publisher(s) alone. Reference to other sources of information does not constitute a referral, endorsement, or recommendation of any product or service. The existence of any particular reference is simply intended to imply potential interest to the reader.

The views expressed herein are exclusively those of the author and do not represent the views of any other person or any organization with which the author may be associated.

INDEX

Page numbers in *italic* denote illustrations

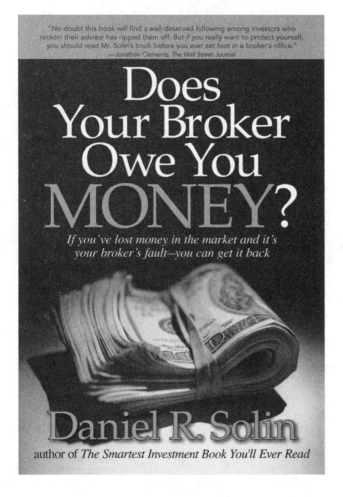